THE CIVIL WAR IN KILDARE

THE CIVIL WAR IN KILDARE

James Durney

MERCIER PRESS

MERCIER PRESS
Cork
www.mercierpress.ie

© James Durney, 2011

ISBN: 978-1-78117-823-2

10 9 8 7 6 5 4 3 2 1

A CIP record for this title is available from the British Library

This book is sold subject to the condition that it shall not, by way of trade or otherwise, be lent, resold, hired out or otherwise circulated without the publisher's prior consent in any form of binding or cover other than that in which it is published and without a similar condition including this condition being imposed on the subsequent purchaser.

No part of this publication may be reproduced or transmitted in any form or by any means, electronic or mechanical, including photocopying, recording or any information or retrieval system, without the prior permission of the publisher in writing.

*For the Gauls of Rathasker Road, Naas,
who lived through the times.*

Contents

Acknowledgements	11
Introduction	13
1. Kildare at War 1916–21	17
2. Evacuation	28
3. The Killing of Lieutenant Wogan Browne	37
4. The Kildare Mutiny	44
5. The Split	58
6. Civil War	73
7. Guerrilla Days in Kildare	91
8. The Great Escape	117
9. 'Seven of Mine,' said Ireland	129
10. Youthful Incendiaries	144
11. Tintown	155
12. Peace Comes Dropping Slow	162
13. Hunger Strike, Murder and Mutiny	169
Conclusion	184
Appendix I	188
Appendix II	195
Notes	203
Bibliography	216
Index	220

War with the foreigner brings to the fore all that is best and noblest in a nation – civil war brings out all that is mean and base.

Frank Aiken, August 1922

Acknowledgements

While this book would have eventually been written I must thank Mario Corrigan for – pardon the phrase – putting the gun to my head and making sure it was written now! My big thanks to the Local Studies, Genealogy and Archives Department, Newbridge, where much of the material and photographs in this book were accessed. My thanks to a wonderful editorial team, Mary Feehan, Mario Corrigan, Gale Winskill and Wendy Logue; as always to Commandant Laing and his excellent staff at the Military Archives, Dublin; my son Brian Durney for the map of Kildare; Karel Kiely, Genealogy Department, Newbridge; James Pooge, USA, for the photos and stories of Jimmy Whyte; Mick Brady, late of Leixlip library; Dan O'Connor, Celbridge; Jim Doyle, Celbridge; the late Paddy Sheehan, Newbridge; the late Marie Maher, Rathangan; Joseph Ua Buachalla, Maynooth; Liam Kenny, Naas; the late Lieutenant-Colonel Con Costello, Naas, always an inspiration; Frank Lawler, Naas, for the photo and story of his father, Peter Lawler; Kenneth Ferguson, *The Irish Sword*; Brian Dunne, Naas, for the photograph of his father, Jimmy Dunne; Seamus Cullen, Donadea; Paul Cooke, Newbridge; John Wogan Browne, Australia; Steve White, UK, and Paul White, Canada, who have kept the spirit of their executed uncle, Stephen White, alive; John O'Reilly, UK, for his reminiscences and photograph of his mother, Annie Moore; Adrian Mullowney, Kildare; and last of all, my wife, Caroline, for her patience and perseverance.

Introduction

The Irish Civil War began on the morning of 28 June 1922 with the bombardment of the Four Courts, Dublin, and ended in May the following year with the republican's 'dump arms' order. There were three main phases in the conflict. The first, from June to the end of August, saw the fighting between the republican (anti-Treaty) and national (pro-Treaty) forces waged largely on conventional lines. The defeat of the republicans in the field led to their re-adoption of guerrilla tactics. With conventional hostilities ostensibly over, the struggle was now carried on by ambush and counter-ambush. In this second phase, a military stalemate ensued which began in September and lasted until December. The third phase began in December and saw the development of an increasingly ruthless, and ultimately victorious, counter-insurgency strategy by the Provisional Government, which responded to a shift in tactics by using the same measures that the British had employed: emergency powers, internment and official and unofficial reprisals. Though victory for the government came in May, with the Irish Republican Army (IRA) order to dump arms, this phase can be considered to have lasted until the end of July 1923, when martial law ended. From August 1923 until mid-1925 a variety of emergency public safety acts were in force, which had a detrimental effect on the remnants of the IRA.[1]

During the War of Independence, County Kildare – as a garrison county with military barracks situated on the main Cork and Limerick roads in Naas, Newbridge, the Curragh and Kildare town – had a low level of republican military activity. Despite this, by the Truce of 1921 Kildare's two battalions had evolved into quite efficient military units. From January 1921, the Kildare IRA increased its activities in what were termed 'small jobs' – the blowing up of bridges, trenching of roads and disruption of communications. The rank and file had become more militant and were pushing for more action. There was talk of forming flying columns from the many men on the run, though many more were behind bars or barbed wire.

When the Civil War broke out in 1922, the county was divided, with the bulk of the activists going anti-Treaty. A surprise raid in the first days of the Civil War by the National Army netted two of the county's main leaders – Easter Week veterans Domhnall Ua Buachalla, TD, and Tom Harris – while another leader, Art O'Connor, TD, was captured in the Dublin fighting. Three young hardliners emerged to lead republicans in Kildare: Jim Dunne and Bryan Moore in the middle of the county, and Patrick Mullaney in the north. Dunne led a column of Volunteers who escaped from Dundalk prison back to Kildare; Moore's Rathbride column operated around the Curragh camp and against Kildare railway junctions in an attempt to disrupt communications to the south and west; Mullaney's column planned to capture Baldonnel Aerodrome and bomb Leinster House by aeroplane.

The Civil War left its mark more violently on the county than the War of Independence; forty-five people in or from County Kildare died during 1922–23, whereas fifteen people died in the 1916–21 period. Kildare has one of the highest figures of IRA Volunteers executed during the war – eight – and the largest single execution of the war took place there in December 1922, when seven men from the Rathbride column were executed at the Curragh. The contrast between the two periods in the county overall was great: seventeen National Army soldiers were killed in ambushes in the county, yet only three policemen died during the Civil War, while no British soldiers were killed in the 1919–21 period; two internment camps – Tintown and Newbridge – housed nearly 3,000 prisoners in 1922–23, while in 1921 the Rath camp held 1,200. The internment camps were the scenes of shootings, executions, murder, mass hunger strike and huge jailbreaks – an escape from Newbridge being the biggest in republican prison folklore, with 112 prisoners getting away. Two 'big houses' were also burned down – Lord Mayo's 'Palmerstown' and General Mahon's 'Mullaboden' – as the 'young incendiaries' blazed a trail of destruction across the county.

1

KILDARE AT WAR 1916–21

At the dawn of the War of Independence period Kildare was a garrison county with military barracks situated on the main Cork and Limerick roads in Naas, Newbridge, the Curragh and Kildare town. The presence of the military had been a great boon to the county and the town of Newbridge had practically sprung up around the military barracks. It was very different from the days of 1798 and the Emmet Rising of 1803 when Kildare was considered to be a disaffected county. Kildare's proximity to Dublin ensured its national strategic importance in the 1798 and 1803 rebellions, and even after Robert Emmet's rising the county presented a continual problem for Dublin Castle. The Lord Lieutenant, the Earl of Hardwicke, commented after the July 1803 rebellion:

> I am sorry to say that such has been the state of the county of Kildare since the rebellion of 1798 as to require at all times the particular attention of government, and there is a more general and rooted spirit of disaffection in that county than any other part of Ireland.[1]

The crown's solution to the problem of Kildare – and as a deterrent to a French invasion – was to build military barracks on the main Dublin to Cork and Limerick roads: at Naas in 1813; Newbridge, 1819; the Curragh, 1855; and Kildare town, 1901. Kildare became a garrison county, tied to the British military presence economically through its trade, and loyally through the integration of the military with the civilian population. While Kildare was a reasonably prosperous county in times of economic hardship, particularly around its urban centres, the county became a major recruiting area for the British army. With an average of 10,000 British troops in the county, the possibility of a military confrontation between rebels and crown forces could only end the same way it had in 1798 – in defeat. However, there were other ways to confront the crown.

County Kildare, up until recently, has received bad press for its part in the War of Independence. The implication was that this area had under-performed during that time in the crucial disruption of communications, the activity to which it was best suited.[2] Physical and geographical factors affected performance: Kildare is the flattest county in Ireland, where the greatest eminence is often a hump-backed railway or canal bridge. The open flat plains of Kildare militated against ambushes, while its proximity to the capital also inhibited the Kildare IRA. There was also the fear of bringing retaliation on their communities. (The three main attacks in Kildare – Greenhills, Maynooth and Barrowhouse – brought immediate reprisals from the forces of the crown.) There were roughly 40,000 British troops and 10,000 armed police in Ireland, and while the IRA could not militarily defeat them they could make the country ungovernable.[3] The Kildare IRA was heavily outnumbered by crown forces and had neither the manpower, nor weaponry, to seriously challenge them. With about 300 activists in the county, and only about a third of them ready to take to the field at one time, the Kildare IRA faced nearly 10,000 troops and hundreds of police, including a company of Black and Tans based at Naas, coupled with a huge population of ex-servicemen and families tied to the military.[4] However, the county was an important axis for intelligence gathering and communications to the south.

Within weeks of the formation of the Irish Volunteers in November 1913, units of this new force had sprung up in nearly every parish in the county of Kildare. While a substantial part of the population was still loyal to the crown there was a major revival of nationalist feeling and, by August 1914, the strength of the Irish Volunteers in County Kildare stood at 6,000.[5] However, when the Volunteer movement split, only five companies – Naas, Maynooth, Kill, Prosperous and Athgarvan – remained loyal to the Irish Volunteers along with the auxiliary organisations, Cumann na mBan and Fianna Éireann. British intelligence believed the number of Irish Volunteers in Kildare to be 344 men, armed with about twenty-four rifles. In the autumn of 1915, Dr Ted O'Kelly from Maynooth was appointed by the Volunteers' GHQ (General Headquarters), in Dublin, as the head of the movement in Kildare.[6] O'Kelly had the hard task of reorganising the Volunteers and preparing them for an insurrection against British rule.

When the mobilisation order for the 1916 Easter Rising – and subsequent countermanding order – reached County Kildare, the conflicting orders caused the same amount of confusion as they did in every other part of the country. However, several companies mobilised and some men made their way to Dublin to take part in the fighting. As part of the general uprising, GHQ expected the Kildare Volunteers to provide 100 to 150 men to demolish railway lines, roads and other communications between Dublin and the Curragh. The Royal Irish Constabulary (RIC) barracks at Sallins and Kill were to be attacked, but as there were only five under-strength companies in the area, the plan was abandoned. The main plan was to destroy the railway bridge over the canal outside Sallins to prevent troops from the Curragh getting to Dublin.⁷

When few Volunteers turned up for the Rising, Ted O'Kelly and Tom Harris (Prosperous) made their way to Maynooth and joined Domhnall Ua Buachalla and twelve other local Volunteers who marched to Dublin to take part in the fighting. The Kildare men joined the GPO garrison on Tuesday and fought there and in Parliament Street, until the garrison's surrender on Saturday 29 April. There were other men from Kildare involved in the Dublin fighting, including Frank Bourke (Carbury) and Jim O'Neill (Leixlip), who also fought in the GPO. (Jim O'Neill later became leader of the Irish Citizen Army.⁸) A Citizen Army volunteer, George Geoghegan, born in the Curragh, was killed in action on 26 April in the City Hall fighting.⁹ Other Volunteers attempted to get into Dublin, but could not get through the British cordon.

The only physical evidence of the Rising in Kildare was the hold-up of a police patrol in Maynooth and the cutting of a telegraph pole on the railway line between Kildare and Athy.¹⁰ During, and in the immediate aftermath of, the Rising, twenty-eight men who did not take part in the fighting were arrested in County Kildare. Some were released, but some joined their comrades who were sent to jails and detention camps in Britain. Of the several hundred men interned in Frongoch camp, eighteen were from Kildare. These included all of the Maynooth contingent.¹¹

In early 1917, the Irish Volunteers were reorganised in Kildare and a battalion council was formed. Officers from the following companies were represented at the meeting: Maynooth, Celbridge, Leixlip, Kill, Naas, Prosperous, Newbridge, Athgarvan and Carbury.¹² In the south of the county, Éamonn Malone (Athy) was appointed commandant of Carlow Brigade, which extended into parts of Kildare, Wicklow and Laois, while Éamonn O'Modhrain

(Athgarvan) was appointed OC (officer commanding) 6th Carlow Battalion, which had several companies from Kildare under its jurisdiction. In the aftermath of the Rising, two more companies were formed in Kilcullen and Castledermot.[13]

The rising tide of nationalism can be measured by the results of the 1918 general election when Kildare returned two Sinn Féin MPs. In North Kildare, Domhnall Ua Buachalla (Sinn Féin) received 5,979 votes to John O'Connor's (Irish Parliamentary Party) 2,772. With 13,000 people on the register and 8,855 votes recorded, Ua Buachalla had a clear majority of 3,207, the largest majority ever in North Kildare. In South Kildare, Art O'Connor (Sinn Féin) was elected with 7,104 votes while Denis Kilbride (Irish Parliamentary Party) received 1,545, giving O'Connor a majority of 5,559.[14] In the local elections of 1920, Sinn Féin and Labour – the Labour Party was a strong supporter of the republican ideal – captured the local councils with twenty-eight seats out of twenty-nine. Domhnall Ua Buachalla became chairman of the county council, with prominent republicans, Tom Harris and Michael Smyth, also being elected.[15]

Early in 1920, after an organising campaign by Peader McMahon from GHQ, Kildare was divided into two battalions, 1st Kildare Battalion and 2nd Kildare Battalion – the latter included some companies in west Wicklow.[16] There were approximately 300 Volunteers in Kildare and they were engaged in the many small operations that made up the bigger picture. There were more ways to run a 'war' than outright military attacks. If David Lloyd George's aim was to make 'Ireland a hell to live in', the republican movement's aim was to make Ireland a hell for Britain to govern. In his witness statement to the Bureau of Military History, Vice-Commandant Michael Smyth gave a detailed description of the overall role of the Kildare battalions from 1920–21, painting a picture of continuous activity: raids for arms, attacks on crown forces (planned and implemented, more of the former, however), raids on the mail trains, implementation of the Belfast Boycott, trenching of roads and felling of trees, burning of tax offices and evacuated barracks, and arrests and punishments of law breakers and spies. Commandant Smyth claimed (in somewhat of an exaggeration) that:

> The Kildare Volunteers succeeded in making the large number of crown forces stationed in the Curragh very much less effective than they should have been by their constant harassment of them, by implementing the orders of the Volunteers GHQ and wrecking the enemy lines of communication in every direction.[17]

In their April 1920 campaign against evacuated police barracks and customs offices, Volunteers in Kildare burned barracks at Lumville, Castledermot, Maynooth, Sallins, Donadea, Ballinadrimna, Clane, Kill and Kilteel, while customs and excise offices in Naas, Athy and Leixlip were raided and many records destroyed.[18] Republican courts were also very active. A battalion police officer was appointed and republican courts were set up in the towns in the battalion area. Volunteers were engaged in guarding these courts. A republican court was held in Newbridge courthouse under the pretence of an Irish language class. Scouts were placed outside and, when the RIC raided, the 'students' pulled out their Irish books and proceeded with their 'class'. Patrick Kelly (Newbridge) was the presiding republican judge in Newbridge court.[19]

The IRA endeavoured to curb cattle stealing and keep the peace when they performed police duty during the 1919 Farm Workers' Strike in North Kildare. The strike began in Celbridge with sixty labourers joining the County Kildare Farmers' Association and there was a warning from their employers of a general lock-out.

In the face of this threat the Irish Transport and General Workers Union (ITGWU) coordinated a strike throughout the county, which soon spread to County Meath. Offending farms were blockaded and strikers wielding clubs prevented the movement of goods, boycotted urban suppliers, disrupted fairs and auctions, and engaged in cattle drives and damaging crops. A settlement was agreed on 23 August 1919.[20]

During the local elections in June 1920, Kildare Volunteers were engaged as guards at public meetings and at polling stations. On the military front, Kildare republicans made several attacks on the crown forces and alleged collaborators. Ten people died violently in the county during 1919–21: a policeman died in an attack in Maynooth in February 1920, and another two died in an attack at Greenhills, Kill, in August 1920; two IRA Volunteers were killed in an attack on an RIC patrol near Barrowhouse, Athy, in May 1921; two alleged spies were shot dead by the IRA in 1921; a mother and child were accidentally burned to death in an attack on the army and navy canteen in Ballymany, Newbridge, in July 1921; and a civilian was shot dead by a soldier at Maddenstown, near the Curragh. There were several other unsuccessful gun attacks on crown forces and an aborted ambush on some Black and Tans near Celbridge that led to the arrest of several Volunteers from a Kildare/Meath flying column, which operated in North Kildare.[21] Jim Dunne stated that:

> In October 1920, Capt. P. [Patrick] Dunne asked Commandant T. Harris to allow him to start a flying column in Kill area, as he had ten or twelve men on the run and could arm them. Commandant Harris replied that he had instructions from GHQ that a column in the Kill area would cut the line of communication to the south of Ireland, which must be kept open for dispatches. After this order, the activities

of the company were reduced to blocking roads, raiding post offices, training, etc.[22]

Dunne's disappointment was obvious. He was a dedicated Volunteer, who got his own way during the Civil War when he formed his own flying column, which was responsible for the deaths of at least four National Army soldiers.[23]

In what the republican movement termed 'small jobs', the Kildare IRA performed unsatisfactorily at first, but soon they were carrying these out well enough to receive a commendation from Chief of Staff Richard Mulcahy.[24] Patrick O'Keefe (Kilcock) stated that by 1920:

> IRA duty was almost full-time now, raiding for arms, doing police duty, collecting Sinn Féin Court Fines imposed by the local Boycott Committee ... I was with the Kilcock company at the burning of the RIC barracks Maynooth, Buckley House near the old Barrack, and the Ulster Bank, Kilcock, all on different nights, and the demolishing of all the bridges and culverts in and around Kilcock (we had no way of blowing up anything at that time, just pick and shovel). During those operations I was always given a gun to watch and guard from a vantage point.[25]

In January 1921, the *Leinster Leader* reported on increasing IRA activity in the county in the week ending 15 January:

> The bridges over the Liffey at Celbridge and Straffan were damaged ... At Maynooth the railway bridge and canal bridges were destroyed ... The bridge between Allenwood and Carbury has been destroyed, while along the big stretch of bog between Rathangan (County Kildare) and Edenderry (King's County) a large number of trenches

were dug. In some districts in North Kildare trees were found lying across the road. On Tuesday night last two more bridges were damaged at Kilcock and the roads blocked with trees.[26]

However, it was intelligence gathering that was Kildare's main contribution to the war. Michael Collins had a huge network of spies and agents throughout the country and this was where Kildare played its most vital and important role. The railway men in Kildare were either members of the republican movement or strong supporters. For example, Frank 'Joyce' Conlan from Newbridge, who was working as a railway employee, was an intelligence operative for Michael Collins, and became an intelligence officer for Kildare. Very few knew of his active involvement in the movement. It was only when IRA medals were presented many years later that people found out the extent of Conlan's involvement.[27] His story, like that of many operatives, remained hidden until late in his life.

One of Collins' most important spies was Eamon Broy, from Rathangan, who was a typist in the detective office of the Dublin Metropolitan Police (DMP). From the time of the Rising he passed on information to republicans through the O'Hanrahan family, whose son Michael was executed in 1916. However, nothing seemed to come of his efforts until he met Collins, who understood precisely where the police fitted into the British system. By this time Broy had been a policeman for eight years and brought Collins inside information on how the system worked and how the men were trained.

The DMP was divided into six divisions, 'A' to 'F', along with 'G' which was the political division and investigated anyone thought to be disloyal to the British authorities. Each 'G man' had his own notebook and every night its contents were transferred to a large book in the headquarters of 'G' division in Brunswick Street.

Eamon Broy was a confidential clerk at headquarters and had access to this book. A copy of every secret report also crossed his desk and, subsequently, Michael Collins received copies of anything of importance that fell into Broy's hands.[28]

Collins also had a spy in Naas RIC barracks. Sergeant Jeremiah Maher was confidential clerk to County Inspector Supple at Naas, and passed on details of a new cipher to Collins through Seán Kavanagh, the newly appointed chief intelligence officer for County Kildare. Kavanagh came to Kildare as an Irish teacher for the Gaelic League. He had learned that Maher had passed on information to local Volunteers whose homes were to be raided and he approached him. As a confidential clerk Maher had access to the key of the new police code, the circulation of which was restricted to anyone below county inspector rank. He turned over the key then in use and Collins provided him with wax to make an impression of the actual key that Inspector Supple used to open his office safe. A courier system was established to send written messages to or from Collins within a few hours through the ticket collector at Sallins railway station. The code was changed periodically and a new cipher passed on to each county inspector. Maher had access to each new cipher and passed it on to Kavanagh.

Maher recruited a fellow RIC man, Patrick Casey, who took over Maher's duties whenever the latter was absent on leave or through illness. Maher continued to pass on information and refused promotion in order to continue his work. Realising that suspicion of his activities had been aroused, he resigned at the end of 1920, and was replaced by Patrick Casey, who continued Maher's work. When Kavanagh was arrested on the eve of Bloody Sunday he was replaced by James Clancy from Newbridge. During the whole time the Maher–Kavanagh network operated, Kavanagh was under orders from Collins to have no dealings with the local

IRA. The only man who knew officially of the network was Tom Harris, the Kildare Battalion OC. Kavanagh's intelligence service also received important information from a member of the clerical staff in the office of the crown solicitor in Naas.[29]

The circumstances in the county made it extremely difficult for the Volunteers to operate during the War of Independence. The organisation attracted very few members and its support base was limited, owing to social, economic and what could loosely be termed 'cultural' reasons. It was poorly armed and forced to fight in geographical terrain that was only conducive to guerrilla warfare, and it was faced with a military presence which severely restricted movement and organisation. Yet the Volunteers did operate in the county and, while they did not carry out the type of military operations evidenced further south, they certainly made enough of a nuisance of themselves to pin down crown forces that might have been deployed elsewhere. This was particularly true in the months leading up to the Truce when the number of 'small jobs' escalated. More significantly, the Irish Volunteer Force (more commonly known by this point as the IRA) and its supporters in Kildare seem to have been remarkably successful in the intelligence war and information passed on to GHQ. The code-breaking alone was undoubtedly of great importance to the successful outcome of the War of Independence.[30]

2

Evacuation

In July 1921, a general truce came into effect between the IRA and crown forces and, on 6 December, the Anglo-Irish Treaty was signed in London. The conflict over the Treaty, both inside the Dáil and out, split the country in two. Michael Collins, Arthur Griffith and their colleagues were attacked vehemently, accused of treachery, cowardice and stupidity, and of falling for the duplicity of Lloyd George and his threat of 'immediate and terrible war'. The signatories defended themselves well in debate, stating that they had got more out of England than anyone in Ireland had ever done before, and that the country had not been in any condition to resume the War of Independence. Collins maintained that the Treaty provided Ireland not with the ultimate freedom 'that all nations aspire and develop to, but the freedom to achieve it'.[1]

After much debate, the Treaty was passed in the Dáil on 7 January 1922, with a vote of 64 to 57. Eamon de Valera broke down briefly under the emotional stress, then led his supporters from the Dáil and prepared to fight the coming 'Treaty election' on the basis of a call for the Republic, and the Republic alone.[2] Kildare TDs Domhnall Ua Buachalla and Art O'Connor voted against the Treaty, as did Robert Barton, who represented Kildare/Wicklow.

Barton had signed the Treaty reluctantly in December 1921, stating it was the 'lesser of two outrages forced upon' him.[3] Nevertheless, he was committed to the Irish Republic and later rejected the Treaty. Art O'Connor subsequently lost his seat to C. M. Byrne, who was the only deputy representing the joint constituency of Kildare and Wicklow to wholeheartedly support the ratification of the Treaty. Ua Buachalla said he voted against the Treaty because 'he knew that the people did not understand the Articles of Agreement', and he 'believed that if the people went wrong that was no reason why he should go wrong'.[4] On 14 January 1922, the Provisional Government for the Irish Free State was elected by members of the southern parliament under the chairmanship of Michael Collins, while the government of Dáil Éireann remained in existence under the presidency of Arthur Griffith. The formal transfer of power from Britain to the Provisional Government began two days later with the handover of Dublin Castle.[5]

Once the Treaty was accepted in the Dáil, the British army immediately prepared to withdraw from Ireland. After the ratification of the Treaty, British forces embarked on a process of evacuation that eventually saw about 40,000 soldiers, 7,000 Black and Tans and 6,000 Auxiliaries leave the Free State. The transfer of this number of army personnel and their equipment was an enormous logistical exercise that was largely accomplished within six months under the control of a committee chaired by Winston Churchill.[6] Across the country, barracks were vacated to pro- and anti-Treaty forces and newspapers carried a constant stream of photographs of departing troops and police. Not every section of Irish society celebrated the departure of the troops. Garrison towns had grown accustomed to a heavy dependence on the money spent by British troops in their locality, none more so than Naas, Newbridge, Kildare and the Curragh, home to around 13,000 soldiers.

The British military presence in Kildare had been an essential part of the economic, social and sporting life of the county. The first new barracks to be built in County Kildare was at Naas, to replace the old one at the South Moat. By the time of the 1899–1901 Anglo-Boer War, Naas had become an important military centre and the depot of the Royal Dublin Fusiliers. The second barracks to be built in the county was the large cavalry barracks at Newbridge, completed in 1819. The town of Newbridge gradually grew up around the new barracks, with shops and pubs supplying the demands of the soldiers. England's wars with France and America, and the Peninsular War, as well as the provision of troops for the empire, meant that there was a constant demand for enlistment and trained men. This latter requirement became a major one with the declaration of war against Russia in March 1854, which led to the decision to make a permanent camp on the Curragh plains to train and accommodate 10,000 men. The camp on the Curragh evolved into the largest military station in Ireland, while the building of Kildare town's artillery barracks in the late 1890s brought about the first increase in the town's population since the famine years.[7]

Not everything ran smoothly, however. The 'Curragh Mutiny' occurred in March 1914, when officers on the Curragh offered to resign their commissions rather than move to the north of Ireland to subdue the anti-Home Rule agitation there. However, within a few months this event, which was unique in the history of the British army, was overshadowed by the outbreak of war in Europe. Urgent telegrams were received at the Curragh mobilising the various brigades for action in France. The 14th Brigade left the Curragh in mid-August and played a prominent role in the retreat from Mons. Once again the central Kildare area witnessed a massive military evacuation. Troops departed from all military stations in the county as hundreds more recruits poured into the Curragh and Naas to be trained for Kitchener's new army. By September 1914, 13,000 recruits were busily engaged in preparing for action in Europe. Apart from the departure of the troops from the county a number of the effects of the war were felt immediately: the price of foodstuffs rose, hundreds of horses were needed as remounts for the cavalry and artillery, and recruitment increased. Thousands of local men and boys answered the call and by the war's end over 560 had been killed in action.[8]

With the implementation of the Treaty agreement there began a final exodus of British troops from the barrack towns in Kildare. On 20 January 1922, a large number of Black and Tans left Naas by the evening train. A couple of nights before, they had given a 'big farewell dance at the depot to their friends, and they had a very enjoyable smoking concert' on the following night. The *Kildare Observer* noted that on their departure:

> ... many of the motors passing through Naas towards Dublin during the week bore good humoured inscriptions including 'Goodbye to some of the best' and 'Sorry to leave you' and 'Good luck to Ireland'. The Tans marched through the Main Street, one of them wrapped in a Union Jack, singing 'Good-bye-e-e' and 'Auld Lang Syne'.[9]

On 7 February, the last detachment of the Royal Dublin Fusiliers left Naas military barracks. They marched out through the front gates and down through the town to the railway station. Many of their friends and relations were waiting at the platform to bid them farewell. Their destination was Bordon, Hampshire, where they joined the 1st Battalion.[10] The famous fighting regiment was one of six Irish regiments disbanded in July 1922. Their departure ended over 100 years of links with the British army. Naas military barracks had been completed in 1813 and many British regiments had been stationed there, until it became the depot for the Royal Dublin Fusiliers. Before, and especially during, the Great War this regiment had enlisted many men from the town and surrounding areas.[11]

Finally, on 1 March 1922, the last British troops in Naas barracks – a company of the Leicesters who had arrived from Athlone – handed over the barracks to Irish troops headed by Colonel Commandant Seán Boylan, Brigadier Thomas Lawler and Captain John Joyce. There was no ceremony to mark the occasion as the Leicesters had sawn down and removed the flagpole so that the Irish Tricolour could not be hoisted. (This was a standard British procedure when evacuating foreign barracks.) The new garrison erected a temporary flagpole alongside the main gate.

The departure of the main military force from Naas had left a force of fifty RIC men distributed between the military and police barracks.[12] On 24 March, the Naas police barracks, the headquarters of the RIC in the county, was evacuated. By then there were only about thirty RIC men left as the military barracks had recently been abandoned. The policemen, their personal belongings, baggage and equipment were removed by lorry to Hare Park barracks, at the Curragh, while some were sent to Kildare, before disbandment. Local officers of the IRA were engaged during the day in checking the inventory of property to be handed over to them on behalf of the Provisional Government. There were no well-wishers, only a group of spectators who watched the last of the RIC leave. The *Kildare Observer* reporter stated: 'A few minutes later the Tricolour fluttered in the breeze from the flagstaff over the barracks, which had never previously supported anything but the Union Jack.'[13]

On the same day, a number of lorries with men from Gormanstown depot arrived in Kildare to evacuate the RIC quartered there and removed them to the Curragh. On 24 March, the RIC barracks in Maynooth was also evacuated and the *Kildare Observer* reported that: 'There is, therefore, today [25 March], no police barrack in County Kildare occupied by the RIC beyond the concentration camp at the Curragh.'[14]

May brought the evacuation of the last British troops from the Curragh, Newbridge and Naas, along with violent incidents from republicans. British troops at Ballyfair House came under fire and had to strengthen the garrison. Shots were fired from a train, after it had passed through Newbridge, at British troops on guard behind sandbags at the station. On 10 May, the final orders for the evacuation of the Curragh were issued. The occupation of Hare Park by an advance party of eighty National Army troops took place on the afternoon of 15 May as planned.

The next morning the Irish and British officers met at the staff house as arranged, and in the pouring rain proceeded to formalise the transfer of the camp from British control to that of the Provisional Government. There was no exchange of compliments between both groups, and the British soldiers marched off as the Irish troops approached. Groups of Irish and British officers proceeded to inspect the perimeter of the camp. Then the two remaining platoons of soldiers, from the Northamptonshires, formed up. The 'Last Post' was sounded, and the handover was officially completed. The *Freeman's Journal* of 17 May 1922 reported: 'That the significance of the event needed no emphasising ... there was no ceremony to mark the surrender of this, the greatest of England's military strongholds in Ireland.'

When the Irish troops went to hoist the Tricolour they found that the British had cut down the three flagpoles in the camp. When two Board of Works' men set about repairing them, they were arrested. It was midday before a pole was found and Lieutenant General J. J. 'Ginger' O'Connell, OC, raised the Irish flag on the water tower. Irish soldiers saluted as Desmond Farrell, TD, representing the cabinet, and a number of Irish and foreign journalists, looked on.[15]

'Thanks be to God,' said an elderly spectator of the evacuation, 'there goes the last of them. Now we are free.'

'Yes,' said another, 'free to shoot each other instead of them.'[16] How prophetic his words turned out to be.

Kildare native Hester May, a twenty-year-old Cumann na mBan member, was the only woman present at the historic occasion. Born at Duke Street, Athy, Hester joined Cumann na mBan at an early age and went to work in Dublin as secretary to Piaras Béaslaí, editor of *An tÓglách* (The Volunteer). After Béaslaí departed to the United States, Hester began to work for Ginger O'Connell, then assistant chief of staff of the IRA, at whose invitation she was at the Curragh for the handover. She remembered having to ask her parents' permission – they were dangerous days, she said to a *Leinster Leader* journalist in a 1985 interview.[17] Hester rubbed shoulders with all the leading men of the times and remembered in particular meeting both Michael Collins and Eamon de Valera. Following the end of the War of Independence, Hester became a civil servant and, throughout the Civil War, continued to do essentially the same work on behalf of the Free State Government. She married Joe May, another local republican activist, in 1923. Joe died in 1961, while Hester died in 1998, aged ninety-two.[18]

The evacuation of the Curragh was coordinated with the evacuation of Naas and Newbridge barracks. Newbridge barracks was formally handed over at 10.30 a.m. on 16 May, following which 200 trainee Civic Guards from Kildare barracks were billeted there. (Newbridge RIC barracks, at Henry Street, was the first police barracks taken over in the county.) Again there was no ceremony, except the change of guard. As reported, everything 'passed off in a business manner'.¹⁹ Over 300 vehicles brought the last British troops to locations in the Phoenix Park. Special trains also departed from the Curragh siding and Newbridge. The *Leinster Leader* reported that the departing military convoy from the Curragh took an hour to pass through the town of Naas and that 'there were several machine guns at the ready position and many light armoured cars in evidence'. Crowds of people had turned out along the road to Dublin to witness the passing of the British forces, but few cheered them.²⁰ The *Kildare Observer* reported that:

> Tuesday of the present week marked an epoch in the life of the County Kildare, when there was a complete evacuation of the British military from posts that have never previously been unoccupied. Chief of these places, of course, was the Curragh Camp, which has been the headquarters of the British army in Ireland, and in which at all times anything from 6 to 16,000 troops were quartered. On Monday final movement of troops from the Curragh commenced, a constant stream of lorries passing through Naas towards Dublin … The new army took up its quarters, and the Curragh, associated from time beyond the memory of the oldest inhabitant with the British army, had passed into Irish hands and became the headquarters of the Irish army.²¹

The evacuation of the crown forces from County Kildare caused a breakdown in trade. The first collapse of prices was reported in the local papers on 20 May when the price of forage fell. Hay fetched only £9 a ton instead of the usual £14. Unemployment was felt keenly and Newbridge, built around the military barracks, was 'like a ghost town'. A thousand workers who had served the garrisons had lost their jobs and in North Kildare 3,000 were out of work. A deputation of residents from the Curragh and

Newbridge, led by J. J. Fitzgerald, a member of Kildare County Council, met Michael Collins and several of his ministers. They were informed that the Curragh was about to be reopened by the National Army. By August, the employment of civilians in the Curragh and Newbridge barracks had begun. Kildare Brigade Vice-Commandant and Labour Councillor Michael Smyth, though he approved of the Treaty, did not take part in the Civil War. He acted as a recruiting agent for the civilians employed on the Curragh after its opening by the Provisional Government. Naas Urban District Council asked the Minister for Labour to receive a deputation in connection with the number of persons out of work in the district, on account of the evacuation of the military barracks. Further appeals elicited some monies for public works in the urban area to offset the loss. However, the influx of troops due to the Civil War soon benefited the economy of Kildare.[22]

3

THE KILLING OF LIEUTENANT WOGAN BROWNE

Even though the Truce had been signed in July 1921, elements of the IRA continued to operate aggressively against crown forces and the loyalist population. With the signing of the Treaty and the rift in the republican movement, anti-Treaty IRA units began to mount attacks on departing British troops and police, intervene in local disputes and defy the authority of the Provisional Government. In the first two weeks of February 1922, four policemen were shot dead, several were kidnapped and, in Cork, an attempt was made to kill or capture Brigadier General George Higginson, commander of Cork district, during which his driver was wounded. On the border with the newly formed Northern Ireland, there were several major incidents in which dozens of loyalists were kidnapped and several policemen killed.[1]

On the morning of Friday 10 February, a serious incident occurred in County Kildare, which nearly sparked off another round of the Anglo-Irish war. That fine spring morning Lieutenant John Hubert Wogan Browne walked, as was his custom each week, to the Hibernian Bank, in Kildare, to collect the regimental pay for troops in the nearby barracks. As he returned to the barracks, at the junction of Infirmary Road a car was stopped with its hood up. One of its occupants grabbed the pay satchel. Though completely surprised and unarmed Lieutenant Wogan Browne declined to surrender the satchel, resisted and a brief struggle ensued. One of the car's occupants jumped out and shot the young officer in the head. Lieutenant Wogan Browne died immediately. A soldier on duty at the barracks' gate ran to help the injured man as the robbers drove away.

The killing of Lieutenant Wogan Browne caused widespread horror throughout the county. Alarmed by this murder and other outrages, Secretary for the Colonies Winston Churchill suspended the evacuation of British troops from Ireland. He demanded that Michael Collins arrest the culprits, saying that if the Provisional Government failed to do so it undermined its power to govern a new Ireland, which was understood as a direct threat that the British Government would have to step in.[2] Because of the mounting attacks on crown forces in the south and the escalating conflict in the north, the stoppage of troop withdrawals did not come altogether as a surprise, as it was generally realised that precautions were necessary to prevent disorder from spreading. Under increasing pressure, Collins hurried to London in order to see that the Treaty provisions with regard to evacuation were fulfilled.[3]

At the time of his death John Hubert Wogan Browne was twenty-six and the only son of Colonel Francis Wogan Browne. John Wogan Browne was a veteran of the Great War and at the time a lieutenant with the Royal Field Artillery in Kildare barracks. He was a popular officer and a practising Catholic who often served at Mass. A keen rugby player, Wogan Browne was on the army team, and also played for Lansdowne. A match at Lansdowne Road on the day of his funeral, in which he was to have played, was abandoned. His father, Colonel Wogan Browne, had served for twenty-seven years in the King's Own Hussars, and took an active interest in the life of County Kildare as a justice of the peace and as a member of Naas Urban District Council and the County Kildare Archaeological Society. It was he who had adopted the additional surname of Wogan, to perpetuate the memory of that ancient Kildare family into which the Brownes had married. The Brownes of Castlebrowne outside Clane, and their near neighbours, the Wogans from Rathcoffey Castle, had intermarried in the eighteenth century. The Wogan family had settled in Kildare in the fourteenth century, and Charles II granted the Brownes the forfeited estates of the Eustaces of Clongowes Wood in 1667.[4]

In Kildare town rumours about the killing were widespread, and the local doctor, Laurence Rowan, wrote to the *Kildare Observer* to scotch one story. Acknowledging that there had been hostile demonstrations by the military in the town on the night of the killing, and that civilian traders' passes for access to the barracks had been stopped (thus putting their livelihoods in danger), Rowan said that 'it was quite untrue that civilian witnesses to the murder scoffed at the dying officer'.[5]

Huge crowds, including representatives of the IRA, attended the funeral at St Corban's Cemetery, Naas. All the shops and houses in the town remained closed and shuttered as the funeral procession passed through the town and, according to *The Irish Times*, 'there was every evidence of public mourning and sympathy'.[6] The Rector of Clongowes College and some boys of the school followed the coffin to the grave, an act that touched his father's heart profoundly, coming as it did from those who had inherited the traditions of the ancestral home – the Jesuit Society.

Michael Collins ordered that every effort should be made to capture the culprits, and the IRA, who claimed the assassins were not members, joined the military police in the search. Within days Collins sent Winston Churchill a telegram saying:

> With reference to concluding parts of your wire of 11th instant about murder of Lieutenant Wogan Browne. Have just been notified by phone we have captured three of those responsible for the attack. Everyone, civilian and soldier had cooperated in tracking those responsible for this abominable action. You may rely on it that those whom we can prove guilty will be suitably dealt with.[7]

The three local men suspected of the killing of Lieutenant Wogan Browne were arrested by their own comrades in the IRA. Those who had carried out the deed were themselves IRA men, but it seems that they had acted without the sanction of the IRA, which meant that the intended robbery or the use of deadly force was not authorised. The three men were taken to the home of IRA Company Officer Éamonn O'Modhrain of Ballysax and housed there until a decision was made regarding their punishment. While there, they escaped and left the locality. Apparently those guarding them were much relieved because they knew the men and did not want to be faced with the possibility of delivering them up or shooting them. According to Paddy Sheehan of Newbridge, the men made their way out of the county, possibly to Athlone. Other reports say they joined the National Army, which was at that very moment scouring the countryside for them. What better way to hide out than in the uniform of those looking for you? One of the men was said to have later joined the Civic Guard. However, official sources said that the men were held at Trim barracks and eventually released without trial.[8] The *Kildare Observer* reported on the killing of John Wogan Browne:

About 11.30 on that day in question he called at the bank and received a sum of about £135. He then left the bank and proceeded towards the barracks. At the corner of Infirmary Road a Ford motor car stood. This had previously been hired at a local garage by three men, who had paid 15s., it appears for the use of the car, ostensibly to convey a patient from the infirmary. As Lieutenant Wogan Browne approached the car he was held up by two men, who snatched the money from him and dashed for the waiting car. The lieutenant attempted to grapple with the men for the recovery of the money when, it is stated one of the men sitting in the car fired point-blank at him with a revolver. The bullet passed through his eye and he collapsed on the roadway, death being almost instantaneous. Meanwhile the driver of the motor was told by the three men to drive off as speedily as he could across Infirmary Road and in the direction of Kildoon, revolvers being held to his head. He did as he was bidden, and having covered some few miles the car was stopped in Kildoon bog, the desperadoes dismounted and told him to return to Kildare, which he did. Later military police and IRA united in a search for the miscreants. Several arrests were made later by the IRA police, but so far no proceedings have been taken, although at least two of the men apprehended were detained and conveyed to Naas, where they have since been held.[9]

The death of his son was a crushing blow from which Francis Wogan Browne never recovered and shortly after this he sold his house Keredern (Naas) and left Ireland, never to return. In 1927, Colonel Wogan Browne died while he was on a motoring tour of France and was buried there. With the death of Francis Wogan Browne – the last male representative of an ancient Catholic family – the family name disappeared from Ireland.[10]

At the inquest into the killing, held at the Curragh Military Hospital, it was established that, as reported, the men had hired the Ford car and driver in Kildare for fifteen shillings, purportedly for the conveyance of a patient to the infirmary. Jack Graham, the driver, said that he did not know any of the men, who he described as 'country men', and that he was forced to drive away from the scene of the crime with one of the men holding a revolver to his head. At Kildoon, a short distance from Kildare town, the men left the car, threatening him not to reveal anything. They left with the sum procured – £135.[11] When Jack Graham died in the 1950s he was given a republican funeral. Perhaps, after all, he did know who his three fares had been on that Friday morning in February 1922.

The murder of Lieutenant Wogan Browne soon faded into memory as more violent incidents continued throughout the rest of the month and into April. Republicans fired at a British army officer at Suncroft, near the Curragh, while crown forces came under attack on 20 February 1922, when there were three ambushes on military lorries on the road from Dublin to the Curragh. This caused the British authorities to reinstate pre-Truce precautions and several parties were observed to be carrying their rifles; a course which had not been observed since the withdrawal of the troops began. These attacks – combined with a week-long strike by 2,000 railway men in Cork – halted the evacuation for a short time.[12]

On 28 March, General Dudley was held up by three men at Limerick Bridge and his car stolen as he drove from Newbridge to Naas, while two staff cars were stolen from the Curragh camp.[13] In April, the home of Captain Ernest Northern, Connaught Lodge in Kildare town, was burned down by armed men.[14] When Margaret Chaplin's Leinster Lodge, again in Kildare town, was destroyed by fire, the local IRA issued a statement regarding the burning of loyalists' houses in the Kildare district, saying they had nothing to do with these incidents and stating that if the perpetrators were apprehended 'they will be punished in such a manner as to prevent such cowardly outrages taking place in the future'. Loyalists in the area were informed that should they require any protection whatever for person or property they would be afforded it on making application.[15] At Punchestown races two armed men held up the driver and stole the Crossley saloon of the lord lieutenant, Lord FitzAlan, who was attending the meeting.[16]

In Kill a number of houses in which policemen and former policemen were residing were attacked. Those attacked were Messrs Adams, Vincent and Hayard, ex-RIC men named Lougheed and Minahan, and an RIC man named Hall. The telephone of the Dew Drop Inn was disconnected before the attack on the houses, a number of men went in and having roused the manager, Mr Bowe, ordered him to put out the lights before entering. At Vincent's house the door was smashed in and while Miss Vincent was closing it she was struck with a stone. An invalid elderly woman at Adams' house was also struck with a stone while lying in bed. Minahan discharged a revolver shot when his house was attacked, and as the attackers withdrew a voice shouted back: 'You won't fire at us tomorrow night.' The houses were so badly damaged that the occupants had to leave in the early hours of the morning.[17]

Despite the investigations of the Republican Police into this incident, intimidation continued in the Kill area. A Mr Hassard, living in the building formerly used as a police barracks, was also forced to move out by stone-throwers.[18] The building was occupied on the outbreak of Civil War by republicans, who a week afterwards set it on fire.[19]

4

The Kildare Mutiny

The first crisis of the Civil War was in Kildare military barracks where hundreds of men had gathered to train for the new police force to replace the RIC. It was there that the tensions between recruits who had fought on the different sides during the War of Independence resurfaced and the Provisional Government, already under pressure from those who opposed the Treaty, was faced with a mutiny within the ranks of its fledgling police force.[1] Most importantly, this coup in Kildare was specifically recognised by the government as 'the first overt act of hostility' against it by the IRA.[2]

There was much turmoil in the county during the Truce and Treaty. During late 1921 and early 1922, there was a marked deterioration in law and order as criminals began to take advantage of the absence of any regular police force in the new Free State. Under the terms of the Treaty, the RIC was disbanded and the function of policing was handed over to the Provisional Government, who then came under pressure to provide a replacement police force. A meeting took place in the Gresham Hotel, Dublin, on the night of 9 February 1922, attended by General Michael Collins, Minister for Defence, General Richard Mulcahy, Éamonn Duggan, TD,

Michael Staines, TD, Colonel Patrick Brennan, TD, Commandant Martin Lynch and General Michael Ring.³ Realising that the experience of former members of the RIC was essential in setting up a new police force, Michael Collins had invited a number of former members of the force who had assisted him during the War of Independence to the meeting. Among them was former Sergeant Jeremiah Maher of Naas RIC barracks, who had kept Michael Collins up-to-date over a number of years with the secret codes used by the crown police in correspondence and was an intelligence officer in the 1st Eastern Division. Jeremiah Maher was appointed to one of the sub-committees to organise, train and recruit for the new force.

The formation of the Civic Guards absorbed some of the Irish Republican Police which had been formed in June 1921, a force which Michael Collins did not admire. Collins wanted a professional police force, not one like the Republican Police 'and the awful personnel attracted to its ranks'.⁴ The original decision to set up an armed police force, the wisdom of which was disputed from the beginning, was soon reversed. The central idea shifted to the formation of an unarmed and non-political police force, in contrast to the heavily militarised RIC, and based on the unarmed and apolitical city constabulary, the Dublin Metropolitan Police. The new police force would have different rank titles, badges and insignia and a dark blue uniform. The police would largely be armed only with a baton, although some would have revolvers. An advertisement in the *Irish Independent* on 7 March 1922, announcing the formation of a police force called 'An Garda Síochána' (Guard of the Peace) or 'Civic Guard', gave rise to the name by which the new police force was destined to be known.⁵ The first commissioner was a pro-Treaty Dáil deputy, Michael Staines. The principle of separating the policing and government functions had not yet quite caught on.

As the political climate deteriorated in early 1922, it became clear that anti-Treaty elements were attempting to penetrate the new force, most of whose members were, after all, former IRA men.[6] Over 6.5 per cent of recruits in Kildare were RIC veterans, mainly Collins' spies and those who had resigned or had been dismissed for patriotic reasons, as well as those who had been in the force when it was disbanded. About half of this group had taken the Dáil side in the War of Independence. With the notable exception of Patrick Brennan and one or two others, Staines appointed RIC men to almost all the influential positions in the new force: District Inspector Patrick Walsh, formerly of Letterkenny RIC, became deputy commissioner and depot commandant; Superintendent Jeremiah Maher became private secretary. The handful of superintendents and chief superintendents of the new force included six RIC men appointed in February and March.[7] The appointment of so many ex-RIC men above the heads of former Republican Police and Volunteers who had borne the brunt of the fighting, caused much dissension in the ranks of the fledgling police force. Eventually, only 129 former RIC men joined the new police force, but rumours persisted that there were 'Black and Tans in the Civic Guard'.[8]

Garda Síochana
(CIVIC GUARD).

The Appointments Office for Counties Kildare and Carlow will be opened on MONDAY, 13th inst., at THE COURT-HOUSE, NAAS.

Intending Recruits should present themselves at the Office between 10 a.m. and 1 p.m. on week days.

Members of I.R.A. will attend on special days by arrangement with Batt. Commandants of all Battalion Areas in the two Counties.

All communications to be addressed to—

Appointment Officer,
Courthouse, Naas.

Recruitment notice from the Kildare Observer, *11 March 1922. (Photo: Local Studies, Genealogy and Archives Department, Newbridge Library)*

Staines was an RIC man's son from County Mayo and had been in the GPO in 1916. His then Deputy Commissioner, John Kearney, had, as an RIC district inspector, been present at the arrest of Roger Casement, a fact remembered by many of the new recruits. Staines surrounded himself with many other ex-RIC men and there had been some discontent in Ballsbridge in mid-March when a group of recruits complained of the presence of RIC men in influential positions. Brennan had promised them that it was only a temporary arrangement and the former RIC men would soon be dispensed with. However, the trend was accelerated in Kildare. At a government meeting on 10 April, Éamonn Duggan, TD, had suggested that the artillery barracks in Kildare might be suitable as a depot for the new Civic Guard, who were at that time housed in the Royal Dublin Society (RDS) showgrounds.

A founder member of the Civic Guard, John McFaul, recorded that on 15 April 1922 an advance party of Guards (including himself) left the RDS showground at Ballsbridge. The group of nearly 300 men travelled by train to Kildare. The party marched from the railway station to the artillery barracks where they took over from the British troops. They were later joined by about 600 new recruits when the RDS premises were evacuated on 25 April and the aspirant policemen marched across the city to Kingsbridge station, where a special train brought them to Kildare.[9] There was a deep contrast between the attire of the new custodians of the law and the retiring crown forces. All the new Civic Guards, including Commissioner Michael Staines, Assistant Commissioner Patrick Brennan and Camp Commandant Joe Ring, were in 'civvies' as new uniforms had not been tailored. They carried Lee Enfield rifles with bayonets fixed. The British wore full khaki uniforms.[10]

The section of the barracks which the Guards were to occupy had been used as stables by the British. The accommodation consisted of British army corrugated-iron huts with hand basins. They were uninhabitable when the Guards found them and for two nights the advance party had to sleep on the barrack square under their greatcoats. National Army troops had also moved into the barracks and their OC placed sentries to keep an eye on these men who described themselves as policemen of the new state. Finally the Guards snapped and let off a few rounds over the heads of the sentries, who hastily withdrew.[11]

The camp was divided into eight lines of huts running parallel to each other and the new recruits formed themselves into companies of around 100, with a company to each line. The recruits engaged in drill instruction, police duty classes and some instruction in the Irish language. There were route marches as far as Newbridge and Monasterevin, which were led by a newly formed Civic Guard pipe band. Football matches took place and even a sports day was held. However, within a few days of their arrival they came under attack from anti-Treaty forces operating in the area.[12] On 18 April 1922, a sentry on duty at the front gate of the army barracks was fired on from a nearby building, while at about 2 a.m. another sentry noticed a group of men in extended formation advancing across a field and, having called on them to halt with no response, he opened fire. The group dispersed.[13]

Recruits continued to flock to the Civic Guard at an average of about 130 a week, so that by mid-May the former military barracks was home to 1,500 recruits. Most of the recruits came from the south, from areas where much of the fighting had taken place during the War of Independence. Of the pre-mutiny Civic Guard, twenty-nine of the 1,488 Guards recruited were from County Kildare.[14] The appointments office for Counties Kildare and Carlow, for the examination of recruits, was opened in Naas courthouse on 13 March. During the first week of recruitment, dozens of applicants were passed for examination at headquarters. Officers were to be selected from the ranks of recruits showing special aptitude and ability.[15]

Some of the ex-Volunteers had been mistreated by the RIC and found it hard to absolve even policemen who had served the national cause. Putting former RIC officers in charge of men who had previously fought against them was very hard for the men to understand. Two former RIC men were discovered in the ranks while the force was in Ballsbridge: John Kearney, who had been a head constable in charge of Tralee barracks when Roger Casement was arrested; and the other was an alleged former Black and Tan. The Black and Tan went over the fourteen-foot-high gate in his pyjamas and ran off with shots hitting the ground at his heels, while Kearney's life at the RDS was made miserable and he spent most of his time in his office guarded by armed sentries. Kearney had, in fact, befriended Casement, but rumour spread that he was the betrayer of the patriot and finally, in the middle of April, he resigned and left for England. However, another ex-RIC man, Patrick Walsh, filled the vacant position.

Kearney's departure was a victory for the IRA men and there was a temporary relief of tension at Ballsbridge. Nevertheless, when the Guards arrived at Kildare barracks, levels of resentment and anger remained high and, when the promotion of five more RIC men was announced on 11 May, they finally overflowed into open mutiny.[16]

The tension between the new recruits and former RIC members continued to develop in Kildare barracks and the recruits began to give them a hard time, obeying them but not showing them 'much respect'.[17] Matters came to a head on 15 May, when Thomas Daly, a veteran IRA man from Clare who had emerged as leader of the disgruntled faction in Kildare, presented an ultimatum in writing to Commissioner Staines demanding the expulsion of five officers, all former RIC men, including Jeremiah Maher. Faced with a direct challenge to his authority, Staines ordered a general parade for two o'clock. The entire depot, around 1,500 men, formed up on the square. Staines read out the ultimatum and called on the eight signatories to step forward. A shouting match broke out between Staines and his supporters and the followers of Thomas Daly.[18] Suddenly, there was a surge forward and Staines moved back, calling for those who stood by him to move to his right. Chief Superintendent Joe Ring, another IRA veteran from Mayo, with about sixty men stood stock-still. Another sixty or so moved to the right with Staines, but the overwhelming majority of the 1,500 men on the square moved to the left. There was half a minute of tense silence and then Staines and his aides backed away to their offices, leaving Ring to restore order. However, Ring could not restore order and he, too, left the square, followed by some of his followers from Mayo.[19] The recruits decided to keep drilling and a committee which had been selected to negotiate with Staines had discussions with the few officers who remained on terms acceptable to both sides, while the commissioner and his staff remained locked in their offices.[20]

The following morning, around 350 men of 6 Company, Kildare depot, boarded a convoy of cars and proceeded to Newbridge, amid shouts of defiance from the Daly faction. Having supervised the occupation of Newbridge, Commissioner Staines returned to Kildare barracks, where he was informed that the Daly faction was planning to seize the armoury. Staines contacted the National Army at the Curragh and requisitioned a lorry to bring some of the arms from Kildare barracks to the Curragh. Daly took control of the depot and distributed arms to about 300 men. Shortly after, Staines quietly left for Dublin, accompanied by around a dozen of his followers, including Jeremiah Maher. In Dublin Staines informed Collins and Duggan of the mutiny and proffered his resignation, but it was not accepted.[21]

With the depot in the hands of the 'rebels', Joe Ring barricaded himself in his room with members of the Mayo faction as Daly awaited orders from the anti-Treaty faction. That afternoon two armoured cars arrived from the Curragh to collect the depot's arms, almost precipitating the first battle of the Civil War. Dozens of Civic Guards armed with rifles and revolvers rushed to the gates to prevent the armoured cars' entry. Commandant Ring ordered the troops to open fire on the mutineers. Captain Corry, the officer in charge of the National Army troops, threatened to force the gates. The Guards ran for cover as Corry cruised up and down the road outside.[22] Superintendent Seán Liddy said: 'We were all within, armed and had instructions to defend our posts. This serious situation had all the appearances of ending in a very bloody scene, but happily it was averted through the intervention of a local priest …'[23]

Eventually, assured that the men had not gone over to the anti-Treaty side, Corry withdrew and the tension eased. On his return to Kildare, Commissioner Staines was refused entry to the depot and had to return to Dublin. The mutineers set about regularising the camp and the committee drew up a proclamation and issued routine orders for the running of the camp. The proclamation was posted up at the gateway to the camp. It read:

> Whereas five persons holding senior commissions in this depot (disbanded and ex-members of the Royal Irish Constabulary) were retained against the wishes of the members of the Civic Guard, and whereas the presence of these five persons was not conducive to the good order and discipline of the depot we requested their expulsion and pending the decision of the Provisional Government we found

it necessary for the peace and good order of the depot to take over temporary control.

We declare our loyalty and the loyalty of the members of the Civic Guard to the Provisional Government and Dáil Éireann.

By order of the Committee.[24]

The men in Kildare appointed their own senior officers and Assistant Commissioner Patrick Brennan became the new commissioner. He had a loyal following of over a quarter of the men and immense influence with the rank and file, and sought to govern and administer the barracks as if all was normal. On 25 May, Arthur Griffith, Éamonn Duggan and Kevin O'Higgins left for London to explain the de Valera–Collins pact to the British cabinet. Collins, who followed a few days later, remained at home to attend personally to the crisis in the Civic Guard. The situation had become so serious that Collins went to the Kildare depot the next day to seek a settlement.[25] The crisis had degenerated so much, he told the men, that as leader of the government he considered it necessary to visit the depot himself. He advised the mutineers to withdraw the offending document and resume their discipline, adding that they had hoped for great things from the Civic Guard:

> A higher standard of discipline is required in a police force than in any other body. It is your duty to enforce discipline on others, and to show by your example that you are fit persons to do so. When you leave the depot, you will be scattered over the country in small bodies, removed from the immediate control of your higher officers ... It is up to you to train and discipline yourselves that when you go out amongst the people your conduct will contrast favourably in every way with that of the force whose place you are filling. You will have

one great advantage over any previous regular police force in Ireland … You will start off with the good will of the people, and their moral support in carrying out your duties. You will be their guardians, not their oppressors; your authority will be derived from the people, not from their enemies …'[26]

Collins promised the men an inquiry, proposing that in the meantime Commissioner Staines and his staff should return to their posts in Kildare. Daly agreed, on condition that a party of not more than five officers return. On 9 June, Staines again presented himself at the depot gates and was again refused entry. Later in the day Superintendent John Byrne and Sergeant Patrick McAvinue arrived from Dublin by train. Byrne was a former IRA Volunteer, while McAvinue had resigned from the RIC in 1918 and was involved with the Republican Police. However, coming from Dublin just after the Staines' visit, the appearance of two more police officials, whatever their political affiliation, rekindled the mutineers' anger. Byrne and McAvinue had to make a quick retreat, followed by armed Civic Guards and dozens of townspeople shouting insults. In the melee one of the Kildare Guards, Sergeant Patrick McNamara, drew his revolver and fired a shot narrowly missing Superintendent Byrne. McAvinue then drew his revolver. People ran to get out of the firing line, while a section of the crowd sang 'The Bold Black and Tans'. The two policemen were pelted with stones as they ran from the scene. As McAvinue tried to make a phone call in the Railway Hotel, the crowd outside threatened to burn down the building. The manager pushed them out the back door and they escaped to a nearby house where they hid in the attic. Later, they were chased by armed men, but found sanctuary in the Carmelite church at White Abbey. They returned to Dublin the next morning by train.[27]

At this stage, Newbridge military barracks was also being used as a training depot for the Civic Guard. The government viewed the recruits in both Newbridge and Kildare as mutineers and, having abandoned any plans for military action after the failure of the army to secure the arms in the Kildare depot, it adopted a policy of isolation and deprivation. Rival headquarters and a recruitment centre were set up in Dublin and all pay was cut for Kildare for the duration of the mutiny. Morale among the men deteriorated. Some left, taking their rifles with them, and joined the anti-Treaty forces; others simply went home.[28]

On 17 June, Thomas Daly, president of the disgruntled faction in Kildare known as the Men's Committee, met a force of anti-Treaty men from Dublin outside Kildare town who accompanied him to the barracks and, using the password, gained entrance, tied up the Guards on duty and commandeered 167 rifles and 243 revolvers, as well as an amount of ammunition from the armoury. A small number of the mutineers joined them and returned to the Four Courts in Dublin, which was garrisoned by a force of anti-Treaty IRA men, but the majority of the men remained in the depot and were faithful to the government.[29] The matter was discussed in Dáil Éireann:

> Rory O'Connor, Ernest O'Malley and Thomas Barry, with an armoured and Lancia car, and a force of Irregulars from the Four Courts, held up members of the Civic Guard, disarmed them, and took possession of their arms at the Cross at Kildare. The disarmed Civic Guards were informed by the O'Connor-O'Malley-Barry party 'they had declared war on England, that they had issued an ultimatum for Monday morning, and that they did not want to be fighting with Irishmen', and they asked the Civic Guards 'to come along with them'.[30]

This incident acted as a catalyst in settling the dispute. President Arthur Griffith and Éamonn Duggan arrived at the depot on 24 June with the following proposals: the men were to be paid all money due to them for past services; an inquiry was to be held immediately; in the meantime all men were suspended. These proposals were accepted and the mutiny was over.[31]

The men were paid a short time later and made up for six frustrating weeks of deprivation with much drinking and revelry and firing of revolvers. One tragic result was the accidental fatal shooting of a young Leitrim recruit, Farrell Liddy, by another recruit who was his neighbour and friend, in the main street in Newbridge. Michael McKenna claimed that he saw a group of 'suspicious men' and when he tried to draw his revolver from his hip pocket it discharged, fatally injuring his best friend.[32]

Although they were suspended, the men, in good spirits with their pay restored, stayed on in the Kildare and Newbridge depots. While life carried on as before, all weapons and ammunition were handed in. The disarming of the police had begun.[33] In the confused aftermath of the mutiny, some of the principal actors – those who threw in their lot with the anti-Treaty faction, and perhaps 350 young men who were disillusioned by the events of May and June – left Kildare quietly and did not return. A strength of 1,500 men early in May fell to 1,150 in mid-June; by mid-July the number was 1,170, and thereafter it increased progressively week by week.[34] However, very few ex-RIC men were recruited to the Civic Guard after the mutiny.[35]

As a result of the Kildare mutiny the Civic Guard could only be employed in pro-Treaty areas. While groups of Guards were sent to the Kildare–Newbridge area on semi-military-type duty as early as mid-July 1922, it was over a month before the first civilian-type police stations began to be opened.[36] The Civic Guard did not occupy the police barracks in Naas until 28 September, when a group of twenty-five – three sergeants and twenty-two guards – arrived in full uniform, and attracted a large group of onlookers. The men were unarmed, but equipped with the baton, as worn in the old days by the RIC.[37] By this stage, General Eoin O'Duffy had taken over as chief commissioner and through his tact and organisational ability the internal dissension that had existed gradually disappeared and the Civic Guard was established on a firm footing.[38]

An inquiry was held into the mutiny in July 1922 and reported that the infiltration of the Civic Guard and the seizure of its arms by anti-Treaty forces had been planned from the time the Guards were stationed in Dublin. It also reported that the extensive use of RIC men 'was unwise'. While the commission's findings laid the major blame for the problems on the mutineers, they pointed to sundry weaknesses within the organisation. The commission concluded that the force should not have been armed and that Michael Staines, as a TD, should not have been appointed to a senior post; it also criticised the leadership's handling of the alarming disorder within the force. The inquiry found the trouble appeared to have originated among the officers and had influenced only a small proportion of men.[39]

The Garda Síochána (Temporary Provisions) Act 1923, enacted after the creation of the Irish Free State on 8 August 1923, provided for the creation of a force of police to be called 'An Garda Síochána'.[40] Under Section 22, the Civic Guard was deemed to have been established under, and to be governed by, the Act. The law therefore effectively renamed the existing force. The new Free State set up the Criminal Investigation Department (CID) as an armed, plain-clothed counter-insurgency unit. It was disbanded in October 1923 and elements of it were absorbed into the Dublin Metropolitan Police. In Dublin, policing remained the responsibility of the DMP (founded 1836), until it merged with An Garda Síochána in 1925.⁴¹

During the Civil War the Civic Guard tried, quite successfully, to remain neutral, and concentrated on the everyday policing of the country. About 100 volunteers, who were anxious to prove their loyalty, formed a Civic Guard Active Service Unit and patrolled the railways in County Kildare by day and night. On Sunday 16 July posts were established at the railway stations in Newbridge and Monasterevin, in the towns of Kildare and Monasterevin, and later at Cloney, Duneany, Portarlington and Athy.⁴² Early in September the unarmed Civic Guard began to deploy to police barracks throughout the country, Naas being one of the first. A long, troubled winter lay ahead as bands of anti-Treatyites, seeing the Guards as a symbol of the state, attacked isolated police units and burned and bombed their barracks. In County Kildare, Athy, Castledermot, Celbridge, Clane and Naas came under attack. The campaign intensified in the new year as the county was scourged by 'an orgy of crime which inevitably follows on decay of ordered government', with attacks on police barracks, railways, roads and bridges and post offices.⁴³ In the tradition of the country, the people would not have given their support to an armed police force and the Civic Guards persevered 'not by force of arms or numbers but on their moral authority as servants of the people'.⁴⁴

In March 1924, the Kildare area was to be the setting for another mutiny, this time in the fledgling National Army. The unrest stemmed from exactly the same cause as that of the Civic Guard, the recruitment of ex-British soldiers into the force, as well as the reduction in strength of the army. It is estimated that some 250 former British officers alone transferred to the National Army.⁴⁵ No lesson, it seemed, had been learned from the police mutiny.

5

THE SPLIT

As the crown forces evacuated army and police barracks throughout the country they were being replaced by either pro- or anti-Treaty troops depending on the area or circumstance. Troops or units who declared for acceptance of the Treaty were armed, uniformed and paid by the Provisional Government, thus forming the nucleus of the 'National' Army, with its headquarters at Beggar's Bush, the first barracks handed over to the IRA. Anti-Treaty leaders regarded this as a betrayal of Richard Mulcahy's undertaking that the IRA would be maintained as the army of the republic. The seeds of a military struggle were being sown and an air of hostility began to emerge throughout the country, as the anti-Treatyites began to make their presence felt.[1]

The Free State or National Army was officially established on 31 January 1922, in Beggar's Bush barracks, and began training troops to be dispatched around the country. The National Army consisted of units almost entirely from Dublin, Leinster and Ulster, as well as new recruits from the ranks of the unemployed. Not only did the majority of the IRA go anti-Treaty, but many also retired from the republican forces. Only those agreeing to support the Treaty were admitted to the new army, though there was a policy of infiltration (to try to unify the army) by anti-Treatyites up to the Army Convention in March 1922. The first regular unit of the National Army consisted of reliable Dublin men who took over Beggar's Bush barracks in March, having been installed earlier in Celbridge barracks.

J. J. O'Connell, as the deputy chief of staff, believed that a small national force should consist of old reliable IRA men and that their task should be to build up a line of stable garrisons, preventing any spread of anti-Treaty areas. Barracks in Limerick, Templemore, Naas (which was to be used as a training base) and Kilkenny were to be taken over by reliable troops, even if that meant going back on Mulcahy's promise to hand over barracks to local IRA units, regardless of their political allegiances.[2]

As early as January 1922, the split in Kildare became evident when 250 people attended a meeting of the Naas Sinn Féin Club, chaired by Father P. J. Doyle, to ratify the Treaty. Father Doyle considered it important that a proper expression of opinion should be given by that group, as it was the club of the county's principal town, and – according to him – had the largest membership in County Kildare, with a roll of over 400. Father Doyle, an avid supporter of Michael Collins and the Treaty, was not disappointed: Naas Sinn Féin voted overwhelmingly to accept the Treaty. County Kildare soon followed suit, and with its ratification the local press urged the people to 'stand by the government'.[3] However, there was sizeable opposition. Robert Barton said he 'personally preferred war than signing the Treaty'; he was going to stand by the Republic proclaimed in 1916, as were TDs Domhnall Ua Buachalla and Art O'Connor.[4]

During the six months after the signing of the Treaty, the entire nationalist movement disintegrated. Cumann na mBan was stridently anti-Treaty, while the Dáil, Sinn Féin and the IRA were split: those who had been politicised by the military campaign tended to be anti-Treaty, while those whose experience had been on the civilian or bureaucratic side tended to be pro-Treaty or, at least, moderate. The general staff of the IRA voted for the Treaty by a majority, but the rank and file voted against it. IRA leaders in the north tended to accept the Treaty on tactical or pragmatic grounds, whereas the southerners tended to take a more fundamentalist line. The women TDs all voted against the Treaty. There was a small, but noticeable, correlation between high social status and pro-Treaty voting among Dáil deputies, which made the soldier versus politician aspect of the split more pronounced.[5]

The split in the IRA was evident in Kildare and both sides claimed to be representing the men of 1916. Both factions also claimed to be the legitimate forces of the Dáil proclaimed in 1919, as these letters to the *Leinster Leader* suggest:

> The general public in the area of the 5th Brigade, 1st Eastern Division, IRA, are hereby notified that I will not be responsible for debts contracted on and after 5 April 1922 by any parties calling themselves IRA and not under my command. I will be responsible only for the payment of goods received on requisition forms signed by me or my Quartermaster, Capt. P. Kelly.
>
> The public are also notified that only the troops acting under my command in this area are the official IRA recognised by General Headquarters and loyal to Dáil Éireann.
>
> Thomas Lawler
> Brigade Commandant
> Brigade Headquarters, Naas
> 6 April 1922

A letter from his opposite number on the anti-Treaty side read:

Officers and men under my command are hereby warned against interfering in any way with the persons or property of individuals holding pro-Treaty views; with any public meetings arranged by any such people; or carrying out any raids for arms on private houses. They are hereby commanded to cooperate in every way in preventing any breach of this order, and generally in maintaining peace in their several areas.

Thomas Harris
OC 7th Brigade
Acting under Army Council[6]

Joe Buckley remembers his father, Domhnall Ua Buachalla, being firmly against the Treaty:

One day when I was doing the books with my father these two men arrived, one was called [Michael] Smyth and I forget the other fellow's name, two great Labour men. When the talk got around to politics I remember my father striking the table with a great bang and saying, 'If every man, woman and child in Ireland asked me to vote for the Treaty I won't do it 'cause it is not for the good of the country.' At home he was the quietest man alive, but in politics he was adamant. After the Treaty debate when the majority in the Dáil had accepted the Treaty he was still sure he was right and he travelled all over the country trying to get people to see his point of view. There were some pockets of pro-Treaty people in this area and Father would think nothing of getting into the car and going off to a meeting (I had to go with him because he couldn't drive the car) and there would be blue murder in the streets. There might be murder at a meeting, but he never fell out with anyone after it but stayed friendly with everybody.[7]

General Eoin O'Duffy visited Naas to put the Treaty position before the Kildare Brigade and Battalion officers. While the meeting was in progress, Jim Dunne led six men from Kill Company and two men from Naas (Jim Whyte and Gus Fitzpatrick) in a raid on Naas police barracks. About thirty men of the Naas Company – 'trucers' and not veteran IRA men – held the barracks. Dunne's group entered the barracks by a ruse and captured about twenty shotguns, several revolvers, ammunition and a large quantity of explosives. Dunne had decided not to go to the brigade meeting as he was taking the anti-Treaty side and no amount of talk from O'Duffy was going to dissuade him. He immediately took over Kill barracks, installing a garrison of twenty men. Kill barracks had been abandoned after the incidents in March when the nearby houses had been attacked by stone-throwers.

A report from the 1st Eastern Division, which was commanded by Seán Boylan and comprised nine brigades which covered Meath, Westmeath and Kildare, stated that the entire divisional staff remained loyal to GHQ (pro-Treaty). However, in Kildare, while Commandant Tom Lawler remained loyal to GHQ, Commandant Tom Harris was elected brigade OC on the republican side. Nearly all the pre-Truce companies took the anti-Treaty side, while many of the new companies, formed during the Truce, went over to the National Army. The republican forces numbered about 400.[8]

Men from the South Dublin Brigade took over Kilbride camp, County Wicklow, from the British on 21 March 1922. Lieutenant Pat O'Carroll of Naas was put in charge of twenty-five men and ordered to proceed to National Army HQ, at Beggar's Bush barracks, to be equipped and armed. When they arrived, they were regarded with suspicion, as it was known that their brigade OC, Andy McDonnell, was not in favour of the Treaty. When McDonnell arrived and tried to influence the men in charge to provide his men with arms, they still refused. He then called Lieutenant O'Carroll aside and told him to bring the men to the arms store, where they found an empty lorry, loaded it up with arms and equipment and drove back to Kilbride camp. Tom Watkins of Tallaght, who was in command of Kilbride camp, said:

> We were both loyal to the Republic and a parade of the garrison was ordered to ascertain how matters stood in this respect with regard to the rest of the men. A number of them declared themselves in favour of the 'Treaty'. These were at once disarmed and ordered to clear out, which they did. Neil McNeil next arrived with a Free State force in lorries but he was refused admission to the camp. He explained that he had come with the back pay that was due to us. This we regarded as a ruse to gain admission, and we declined to permit him to enter on any pretext. He did not press his demand for admission any further and returned with his men.[9]

Pat O'Carroll remained on the anti-Treaty side in the Civil War becoming Wicklow Battalion OC. The battalion operated a flying column in the Wicklow Mountains until near the end of hostilities when it was surrounded and captured.

On 26 March, despite the Dáil cabinet's prohibition, the IRA held a convention and passed a resolution reaffirming its allegiance to the Irish Republic. Two days later, the newly appointed Executive of the IRA announced that the authority of the Minister for Defence and of the chief of staff would no longer be accepted. Maintaining that the IRA was the country's only legal army, the Executive ordered all regular members to report to their units and demanded an end to recruitment for the National Army and the Civic Guard. The following month, anti-Treaty forces seized a number of buildings in Dublin, among them the Four Courts, the Kildare Street Club and the Ballast Office. To fund their force, branches of the Bank of Ireland were raided all over the country and a total of £250,000 appropriated. While the IRA and the National Army were cooperating on operations around the border, fighting broke out between them in Dublin, Sligo, Tipperary and Kilkenny.[10]

As the campaign to demonstrate the benefits of the Treaty began, James Dwyer, TD, speaking in Irish at a pro-Treaty meeting in Athy, said 'that Irish soldiers went into the Great War for the same ideal [of complete freedom]. The Treaty gave us absolute control of our national life, absolute control of our money.'[11]

The initial church reaction to the signing of the Treaty seemed quite neutral and cautious, suggesting only that the Dáil 'will be sure to have before their minds the best interests of the country and the wishes of the people'. But with the growing threat of disorder on the part of the anti-Treatyites, it was to change its stance dramatically and many of the Christmas sermons in 1921 were, in effect, pro-Treaty speeches.[12] There were few priests preaching the republican doctrine.

Meanwhile, posters and handbills advertised a 'Great Leinster Rally' for Naas on Sunday 16 April 1922, at which Michael Collins, Chairman of the Provisional Government, was to be the principal speaker. On the day, a platform was erected outside the Hibernian Bank (now the Bank of Ireland) on which, alongside Collins, were Joe McGrath, Minister for Labour, Kevin O'Higgins, Minister for Economic Affairs, and several other dignitaries, including Gearóid O'Sullivan, adjutant general of the National Army, Alderman Michael Staines, TD, and Christopher Byrne, TD. Also on the platform were Father Norris, PP (Parish Priest); Father P. J. Doyle, CC (Catholic Curate); Father James, PP, Moyvalley; Father Fanning, CC, Clane; Father Fogarty, Dominican; Dr Laurence Rowan, Kildare; Simon Malone, Rathangan; P. Phelan, County

Council; H. C. Fay, County Council; C. Harte, Rural District Council; P. P. O'Reilly, Rural District Council; Tommy Patterson, Naas Urban District Council; Stephen Garry, Naas Urban District Council; M. Stapleton, Rural District Council; and several women, including Mrs Kevin O'Higgins.[13]

On his arrival in Naas, Michael Collins was met by representatives of the Naas Urban District Council – D. J. Purcell, chairman, and Councillors Stephen Garry and Tommy Patterson. Father P. J. Doyle, introduced the deputation to Collins. Father Doyle was an enthusiastic supporter of Michael Collins and a friend of both the Collins and O'Higgins families. Mrs O'Higgins before her marriage had been on the staff of Knockbeg College with Father Doyle, as was Gearóid O'Sullivan. D. J. Purcell, the chairman, read the address:

Beatha agus sláinte. On behalf of the Urban Council and people of Naas we tender to you a most hearty welcome on this your first public visit to the town. We appreciate keenly the honour you pay us in having selected Naas as the centre from which to address

---

SAORSTÁT NA h-ÉIREANN.

COME TO THE
Great Leinster Rally
IN SUPPORT OF
The Free State
AT NAAS
On SUNDAY,
APRIL 16th, 1922.
At 3 p.m. (Summer Time)

MR M. COLLINS
WILL SPEAK; also—
Mr JOSEPH McGRATH, T D.; Alderman M. J. STAINES, T D.; Mr. C. M. BYRNE, T.D.; Mr. KEVIN C. HIGGINS, T D.; Mr. GEAROID O'SULLIVAN, T D.

SPECIAL TRAINS FOR NAAS, at greatly reduced fares, will leave:—
Tullow, at .... 11.15 a.m.
Maryborough, at .... 11.5 a.m.
Bagnalstown, at .... 11.10 a.m.
Calling at all intermediate stations.
Return Trains will leave Naas at about 7 p.m.
For Full Time-Tables, see Railway Company's posters.

50 SAORMID DIA ÉIRE.
(b-250)

Advertisement from the Kildare Observer *for a pro-Treaty rally at Naas, 18 March 1922 (Photo: Local Studies, Genealogy and Archives Department, Newbridge Library)*

the people of mid-Leinster. We are proud to have such a distinguished Irishman among us, and express our ardent wish that your work for Ireland in the future will be crowned with the same good fortune and success as in the past.[14]

The Moyanna Pipers Band played through the town as the speakers arrived. The various speakers were all warmly received and when Michael Collins came to speak he was greeted with loud cheers. The listeners were exhorted to return Treaty men in the coming elections. A contingent of the Republican Police was on duty between the platform and the Town Hall to prevent any interference with the meeting; the only interference being a youthful voice at the back of the platform, and well away from the crowd, which once uttered the cry of 'Up de Valera', and was heard no more.

County Councillor Nicholas Travers from Kilcock chaired the meeting. He welcomed Collins, 'one of Ireland's noblest sons and soldiers', to the ancient town of *Nas Na Riogh*. Collins spoke of the Treaty, de Valera's absence from the negotiations, and the subsequent recriminations. He asked:

> What are the proposals being put forward by the opposition in relation to North East Ulster? How do they propose to bring it in [to a Republic], seeing their leader has pledged himself not to coerce it? The people have a right to an answer to these questions.
>
> Developing and enriching ourselves in our own separate civilisations, the civilisation which fits us and is the expression of us, but we want peace and freedom. Security is vital, substantial freedom, secured for the building up of our nation, confidence and strength in ourselves, which will enable us to stand proudly and self-reliantly before the world.[15]

Collins referred to the newly formed Civic Guard and allegations that the Black and Tans were training the Guards. He told the listeners:

> Those organising our Civic Guards are the men who remained in the RIC and the DMP at the daily risk of their lives. I want to pay a tribute to these men, and the important intelligence which they have provided.[16]

Later that evening, Collins, Mr and Mrs O'Higgins, Joseph McGrath, Gearóid O'Sullivan and others were entertained to dinner in the Town Hall, subscribed for by the residents of several districts in North Kildare. About 100 guests attended, including several women, who no doubt revelled in the company of such a charismatic man as Michael Collins. The *Leinster Leader* 'was not afforded an opportunity of being present' and had to rely on an account from the *Kildare Observer*.[17] Father Doyle presided at the top table and, after the meal, proposed the toast to Michael Collins, remarking that he had 'the proud privilege of claiming Mr Collins as a personal friend and in attempting to say anything complimentary of him he might be accused of painting the lily'. This last remark brought on rounds of applause and laughter. Father Doyle compared Collins to 'a great big stout oak tree similar to that under which our ancestors worshipped of old … a man for whom they had the highest hopes in Ireland of the future'.[18]

On returning to Dublin that night, the car containing Collins and some of his colleagues drove to their party headquarters in Parnell Square. As Collins stepped out of the car, a youth approached and fired a revolver at him at point-blank range. Fortunately, the youth was nervous and his aim poor. He was seized immediately, disarmed and conveyed to Mountjoy Jail. A couple of months afterwards, when speaking to Collins, Father Doyle asked him what had become of his would-be assassin and received a curt reply: 'He had a good face, so I sent him home to his mother.'[19]

On 9 April, a Republican Executive was established and new IRA General Headquarters Staff confirmed. Four days later the Four Courts, the seat of juridical control in Ireland, was occupied and established as the IRA headquarters in Dublin. On 22 May, Michael Collins and Eamon de Valera announced a pact for the forthcoming elections. Both sides would contest the elections under a shared Sinn Féin banner relative to their existing strength in the Dáil, and call on the electorate to vote only for pro- or anti-Treaty candidates and ignore the bread-and-butter issues. In effect, it was an attempt to avoid putting the Treaty before the electorate and to avoid an electoral contest.[20]

The pact displeased the British – who feared the setting up of a republic – so they urged Collins to have it abrogated. On 5 June, while de Valera was in Naas urging an audience to support the pact, Collins was repudiating it in Cork. At the meeting in Naas, de Valera, Harry Boland, Austin Stack, E. Aylward, Robert Barton, Domhnall Ua Buachalla and Art O'Connor delivered speeches. The Kilcock Pipers' Band and Droichead Nua (Newbridge) and Timahoe Fife and Drum Bands attended, along with about 3,000 of the public. De Valera asked those who were in favour of the republican programme to vote also for the panel candidates of the opposition, and said that he hoped that those who were for the Treaty would be equally honest in voting for the candidates who were not on their side. The pact had been made in that spirit. In Cork, Collins made a speech which was a direct repudiation of the pact, calling on the electorate to 'vote for the candidates you think best of'.[21]

However, the situation in the north was putting more and more pressure on the IRA to act. By 18 June, it was calculated that the total casualties since 21 June 1921 were 1,766 wounded and 428 killed. 8,750 Catholics had been driven from their employment, while 23,000 were driven from their homes.[22] The Ulster Special Police (who had replaced the RIC), loyalist mobs and murder gangs, carried out this work. Many Catholics fled south of the border.[23]

On the border there were frequent clashes between pro- and anti-Treatyites on one side and British troops and Specials on the other. The republicans and National Army also cooperated on the provision of arms for the fighting in the six counties. Arms supplied to the Provisional Government by Britain could not appear in the campaign because if they fell into British hands it would cause huge embarrassment. Therefore, careful and detailed arrangements were made between the military leaders on the two sides for an exchange of weapons. During the second and third week of June, rifles from Kildare Brigade were shipped north via Beggar's Bush barracks to be used by northern IRA forces. (When northern incapability to use these weapons became evident, training was provided at the Curragh for these men. However, some of them never returned to Northern Ireland, instead enrolling in the National Army or, in some cases, joining the anti-Treaty forces.) The rifles were to be replaced by weapons from the Provisional Government, but the situation in the south then became critical.[24]

Another IRA Convention was held in Dublin on 18 June. Liam Lynch made proposals for unity, which were rejected. Tom Barry then proposed that, unless all British troops left Dublin in seventy-two hours, they should be attacked. When this was vigorously opposed and rejected, about half of the delegates left to join the Four Courts garrison. Twelve out of the sixteen IRA Executive members were now in the Four Courts.[25]

On 16 June, the Irish people went to the polls. There was some intimidation but less violence than expected. With the exception of Castledermot and Monasterevin, perfect order prevailed in Co. Kildare and the election was fought in the most harmonious manner. In Monasterevin a disagreement between pro- and anti-Treaty forces forced the polling booths to remain closed until 3 o'clock in the afternoon by which time most of the farmers who had come to vote at the station had returned home.

However, there was a more violent incident in Castledermot. On the eve of the election, anti-Treaty republicans took possession of the Sinn Féin hall, which was being used as an election room. Throughout election day, a tender of National Army troops provocatively patrolled the street outside the polling booth. The next morning a party of pro-Treaty troops from Carlow barracks arrived in the town for election duty and proceeded to clear the hall. Two revolver shots were discharged and, when the place was cleared, after strong resistance, Volunteer Thomas 'Smack' Dunne was found mortally wounded. The garrison only numbered four men armed with two shotguns. Captain Lawler of the National Army said the shots were fired accidentally owing to a trigger snapping when cocking it for precautionary purposes.[26]

At the commencement of the election for the Kildare/Wicklow constituency one pro-Treaty and four anti-Treaty candidates were presented jointly on the Coalition Panel for election: pro-Treaty candidate Christopher M. Byrne from Glenealy, County Wicklow, and Domhnall Ua Buachalla and Art O'Connor, Kildare, and Robert Barton and Erskine Childers, Wicklow, on an anti-Treaty ticket. Five other candidates were nominated to contest the seats: Hugh Colohan, a brick and stone layer from Newbridge, and James Everett, a trade-union secretary from Wicklow town, representing Labour; and farmers John James

Bergin and Patrick Phelan from Kildare, and Richard Wilson, Wicklow, for the Farmers Party.[27]

The results were not announced until 24 June and there was no doubting the wishes of the Irish people. They voted overwhelmingly for peace. Pro-Treaty candidates polled 239,193 of a total of 620,283 votes cast (58 out of 128 seats); anti-Treaty candidates polled 133,864 votes (35 seats); and Labour (17 seats), Independents (7 seats) and Farmers (7 seats) won 247,226 votes between them.[28] The list of elected members for Kildare/Wicklow was:

Byrne (pro-Treaty)	9,170
Wilson (Farmers)	6,700
Colohan (Labour)	6,522
Everett (Labour)	5,993
Barton (anti-Treaty)	4,735[29]

While the pro-Treaty party was the strongest, it did not have a majority, so the Republican Party held that the outcome should be a coalition government.

However, events soon overcame them. On 22 June, IRA Volunteers assassinated Field Marshal Sir Henry Wilson in London. Wilson was a Conservative politician and security adviser to the six-county administration. A conference of ministers was hastily convened at Downing Street and the blame for the killing was placed on the Four Courts garrison. Winston Churchill warned that, 'if through weakness, want of courage, or some other less creditable reason' the occupation of the Four Courts was not brought to an end, the British government would regard the Treaty 'as having been formally violated'.[30] When the republicans kidnapped General J. J. O'Connell, deputy chief of staff of the National Army Collins was left with little choice.[31]

A decision was made by the Provisional Government to clear the Four Courts.

In Kildare, Fianna Éireann scout James Whelan died on 25 June and was buried the day before the Civil War began. In a show of unity, both sides – anti-Treaty and pro-Treaty – attended his funeral. Within hours this unity was gone. On 1 July 1922, the *Kildare Observer* reported:

> **MILITARY FUNERAL IN NAAS**
> All forces united on Tuesday to do honour to the memory of Mr Jas Whelan, 1st Lieutenant, 'A' Company 1st Battn. Kildare Brigade Fianna-na-hÉireann, who passed away at the early age of 18 years, after some months' illness, at his father's residence, Dublin Road, Naas, on Sunday. A firing party of the Executive forces headed the procession, followed by the Naas Workingman's Band, playing the Dead March in Saul. Then came the hearse, the coffin covered with deceased's uniform, followed by the relatives and his comrades, carrying the wreaths of 'A' Company and the boys of the Christian Brothers' Schools. There was a large and representative concourse of the public. The Rev. Father Tierney, CC, recited the prayers in the Mortuary Chapel and at the graveside in the New Cemetery. Much sympathy was expressed with the parents and relatives in their bereavement. It was the first funeral of a member of the Irish Army in Naas.[32]

It was not the last. Volunteer Éamonn O'Neill, Sallins Road, Naas, died of wounds on 23 August 1922 (it is unclear where or how he received these wounds). Originally, he was claimed as a member of the National Army, but was buried in the republican plot as an anti-Treaty IRA Volunteer. There would be another half-dozen burials before peace once again came back to the area.

6

Civil War

At 4.29 a.m. on 28 June 1922, Dublin awoke to the boom of two field guns as the National Army began its bombardment of the republican garrison in the Four Courts. The two guns, borrowed from the British, were positioned at Winetavern Street and Lower Bridge Street and barely scratched the stone of the huge building. Liam Duffy from Monasterevin, a friend of Liam Mellows, was part of the garrison. During the War of Independence, Duffy had been an officer in the 6th Battalion, Carlow Brigade, and had been imprisoned in Mountjoy, Perth and Glasgow. Now he would again face imprisonment, this time from his former comrades.[1] After two days of continuous bombardment the garrison capitulated, but not before the Central Hall was blown up, which destroyed records dating back 600 years. Fighting spread to the heart of Dublin as republicans took possession of a whole block on Sackville Street. The fighting in the city centre lasted until 5 July. Around 300 people were wounded and sixty-one killed.[2] The city centre lay in ruins, wrecked again by British guns.

The Civil War split families down the middle. The Sheehans from Henry Street, Newbridge, were a republican family and Mick Sheehan and his brother Jim were active during the 1918–21 period.

Jim had first joined Na Fianna Éireann and then became a court clerk in the republican courts. The Sheehans had two uncles who were also involved in the fight for a republic, one as a Sinn Féin judge, the other active in the Republican Police. During the Civil War, Mick took the anti-Treaty side while Jim and his two uncles took the pro-Treaty side. The Kenny family from Rathangan also suffered the same fate, with some members taking opposing sides. A war between friends and comrades was bad enough, but a war between brothers was devastating and it would take generations to heal the rift.[3]

Some activists remained neutral – Collins' Castle spy Eamon Broy and Michael Smyth, vice-commandant of the Kildare Brigade IRA, took no part in the conflict. Others, such as Hester May and Fintan Brennan, continued their civil service work under the new government. Fintan Brennan, a native of Monasterevin district, joined Sinn Féin in 1912, and his activities in the Anglo-Irish struggle led to his arrest by the British and imprisonment in Mountjoy, Wormwood Scrubs and Parkhurst on the Isle of Wight. His release came in 1922 under the general amnesty. With the establishment of the Free State, he became one of the first district court clerks. At that time he was no stranger to court procedure, for he had previously acted as a justice of the parish or Dáil courts, in Monasterevin under Sinn Féin during the British occupation of the country.[4]

Kildare TD Art O'Connor did not approve of the Treaty and when the Civil War broke out he again took up arms and joined the republican leaders occupying the block of hotels in Sackville Street. Oscar Traynor, as OC Dublin Brigade, made the elementary mistake of seizing a number of buildings in Sackville Street on the side farthest from the Four Courts, so that there was no possibility of linking up with the garrison there. The republicans tunnelled into each building, linking them into an impregnable stronghold, or so they believed. Cooped up in this 'stronghold' was much of the republican leadership – Oscar Traynor, Eamon de Valera, who reported to his old unit as a private soldier, Austin Stack, Robert Barton, Cathal Brugha, Countess Markievicz and Art O'Connor. They were courageous leaders but poor tacticians, disorganised and lacking any overall strategy. The National Army surrounded the buildings and for eight days the garrison came under continuous attack. When it was no longer safe to occupy the buildings the republican leaders withdrew. Cathal Brugha, with Art O'Connor and sixteen others, remained holed up in the Granville Hotel. They continued firing until they could no longer remain in the building. Then they had to surrender to save lives.[5]

By the evening of 5 July, most of the republican garrisons in Sackville Street and the surrounding areas had either been dislodged or had surrendered – de Valera had escaped in the back of an ambulance. Apart from intermittent sniping, the only position still active in the street was the Granville Hotel, which had been under artillery fire for most of the day. By 7 p.m. the firing had ceased and the hotel was ablaze. National Army troops set up machine-gun emplacements in the lanes around the building. Brugha ordered his men to surrender as the building was in danger of collapse. He told Art O'Connor to go out and take his comrades with him. O'Connor advanced into the lane, his civilian clothes covered in dust. He waved a white tablecloth as a flag of surrender.[6] Red Cross men standing at Cathedral Street ran quickly towards them, at the same time shouting to National Army troops located in Hickey's to cease fire.[7] There was some confusion as the republicans were arrested and questioned as to the whereabouts of Brugha. It was thought he was trapped in the blazing hotel, but as firemen attempted to break down a door he emerged defiantly, a revolver in his hand, and made a run for the troops surrounding him. There were cries for him to stop but he advanced on a barricade manned by riflemen. The soldiers fired, aiming low, but a bullet severed a femoral artery. Brugha fell to the ground, in a pool of blood. He died two days later.[8]

An eyewitness report from the *Freeman's Journal* stated:

> Meanwhile, the prisoners moved freely in Findlater Lane. Three nurses who had remained with them to the last stood white-faced defiant, fighting hard to stay the flow of tears which welled in their eyes. A wounded prisoner lay on the ground shot in the arm, surrounded by doctors and Red Cross men, who dressed the wound.
>
> At the most fifteen men were taken prisoner – some young boys with Sacred Heart badges pinned to their coats and wearing revolver holsters. A search by the guard revealed no firearms. They had been left in the consuming flames. Muttering fiercely, the captives paced up and down a garage. The strain of the past few days showed in all their faces.
>
> … a National officer [was] ordered to have the prisoners removed.
>
> 'Republican prisoners, fall in,' cried Art O'Connor, and four deep the Irregulars marched away to Amiens street station.
>
> The news of the surrender spread like wildfire in the district, and crowds watched the departure of the prisoners at the street corners.[9]

Art O'Connor and his comrades were marched off to captivity in Mountjoy Jail. He remained a prisoner until well after the Civil War ended.

The arrests of prominent leaders – Tom Harris, on 28 June, and both Domhnall Ua Buachalla, TD, and Commandant Patrick Mullaney of Leixlip on 29 June – struck a huge blow to anti-Treaty republicans in Kildare. Ua Buachalla was imprisoned in Kilcock,

Maynooth and then the Curragh, while Mullaney was imprisoned in Kilcock, Lucan and then the Curragh. Mullaney escaped less than a month later, on 22 August, and led a column in the North Kildare area until his recapture in December 1922.

A number of other major local republicans were also arrested in the first days of the Civil War: Edward Moran, John Breslin, Daniel Brennan, Thomas Doran and Phil Hade.[10] A new brigade staff was formed with Paddy Brennan as OC, Jim Dunne as vice-OC, M. Ryan as adjutant and A. Metcalf as quartermaster.[11] Trees were felled and trenches dug by anti-Treaty forces in roads around Naas, Blackchurch and Celbridge, while the streets of Naas and all roads leading in and out of the town were held by fully armed men of the National Army.

When occupying Sackville Street, Dublin Brigade OC Oscar Traynor had also taken over Barry's Hotel as a centre for mobilisation and dispatched units to posts in buildings commanding the rear of the Four Courts, in Parnell Square, in Capel Street and in other parts of the city. Hotels in Sackville Street became the general headquarters for the remaining anti-Treaty men. The posts on the south side of the city opposite the Four Courts had fallen to the National Army. Traynor's hope was to get 10,000 men from the provinces into Dublin who would seize the barracks and garrison. He believed they would meet little resistance and, with the men of the Dublin Brigade, would keep peace in the city while de Valera insisted on the summoning of parliament. The republicans expected that the Dáil would repudiate those who opened war at Britain's bidding, denounce the Treaty and again declare for the Republic. As the positions in Dublin were fortified, couriers were sent to the divisional commandants, though there was much confusion about who commanded what. Matters had been made worse by the earlier split in the anti-Treaty ranks at the IRA Convention in June, when Tom Barry had wanted to re-start hostilities against the British and had been voted down by Liam Lynch and Cathal Brugha.[12]

On the day the Four Courts was attacked, nearby anti-Treaty forces in Dublin, Wicklow and Kildare were ordered to concentrate in Blessington, in preparation for a move on Dublin. Liam Lynch and a party of officers and men got off a train at Newbridge and hired cars to Kilcullen where they met Commandant W. Byrne, who was in possession of the local barracks. Byrne obtained vehicles to take Lynch and his party to Tipperary, while Lynch instructed Byrne to take his column of thirty-five men to Blessington, where they arrived the next day. Paddy Brennan, OC Mid-Kildare Brigade, was also notified of mobilisation on the day the Four Courts was attacked. He occupied Coolcarrigan House with men of the 4th and 6th Battalions. Commandant Jim Dunne was notified of the Four Courts attack at 2 p.m. and sent men from the 1st Battalion column to Rathcoole to reinforce the Brittas Battalion of the South Dublin Brigade, under John Watkins. Another section reported to Blessington, while the remainder of the column of thirty-five men held Kill village.[13]

Within days, strong republican forces, including 120 men from the Kildare Brigade, had assembled in Blessington awaiting orders to relieve their comrades in Dublin. Among them were brothers Harry and Gerry Boland, Commandant Paddy Brennan, Andy McDonnell, OC South Dublin Brigade, Seán Lemass and Ernie O'Malley, who had escaped after the fall of the Four Courts. These troops waited for orders to attack Dublin. Eventually a column set off to relieve republican forces fighting in the city centre but as they approached Dublin a messenger from Oscar Traynor said he was disbanding his men and the column returned to Blessington.[14] However, more than 1,000 National Army troops from six bases began an encircling movement through the Dublin Hills. As more republicans retreated into Blessington three National Army columns converged on the town: one under Commandant Heaslip, approached from Brittas; another, led by Commandant Bishop, marched eastwards from the Curragh; and the third, commanded by Commandant McNulty, came through the mountains.

A series of defensive positions were set up and elements of the Kildare 6th Battalion went to Ballymore-Eustace to command the Naas approach and the main road from Dublin. However, their armament was nondescript, as the rifles of the Kildare Brigade had been shipped north by Collins via Beggar's Bush and had not been replaced. Tom Derrig, TD, advised Commandant Byrne not to fight and to leave the town of Ballymore. Around 100 National Army troops, under Commandant McNulty, besieged Ballymore on the evening of Wednesday 5 July. There was a sharp exchange of fire as the first National Army troops, led by Commandant Dineen, crossed the bridge. Dineen was wounded in the knee. A reluctance to shoot to kill was evident. The main republican garrison including Commandant Byrne, which had been barricaded in three hotels, escaped and only eight prisoners were taken. An armoured car machine-gunned Ivy House, forcing the eight-man garrison to surrender. In the advance from Carlow, Ballitore, Monasterevin and Ballymore had been taken by the National Army, along with some fifty prisoners. Two days later the National Army troops attacked Blessington. Roads were trenched and mines laid, but the republicans faded away during the day and night and the town was taken bloodlessly. In the fighting in and around the area the IRA had about forty men captured, but none killed.[15]

During the fighting an Irish Air Corps Bristol biplane, one of three just delivered from Britain, crash-landed in a field at Ballycane, Naas. It was most likely on its way to observe the fighting between

Blessington and Ballymore. The observer was injured, but the pilot escaped unhurt.[16]

The road link between Dublin and the Curragh was vulnerable at Naas and the military barracks there came under fire from republican forces that had concentrated in the Blessington–Ballymore–Hollywood area. The *Kildare Observer* reported that:

> On Tuesday night National forces took up position in some houses in Poplar Square and also took over possession of the Technical Schools and Water Tower. The windows of the schools were sandbagged. Men were also posted at many vantage points in the town in preparation, it was stated, for a threatened attack on the town by the Executive forces, which were stated to be in strength in the vicinity of Blessington and Ballymore. The night, however, passed over peacefully, though residents could distinctly hear shooting after one o'clock in the morning, when about a dozen shots were fired, though at a considerable distance from the town.[17]

In the confused fighting around Blessington, Ernie O'Malley and his men slipped through Commandant McNulty's lines, while the Kildare men continued to march westward, fighting as they went, and reached their bases safely.

In the first few days of the outbreak of war there were several incidents in Kildare: a landmine blew up an armoured car near Blackchurch, though there were no casualties on either side and shots were fired on National Army troops near Jigginstown, Naas.[18] There was much sniping in the neighbourhood of the Curragh on the days following the end of the Dublin fighting. Wires were cut on the Curragh road near Newbridge, and horses and carts conveying food were captured. In one incident, Captain Fitzgerald and Lieutenant Casey of the National Army were wounded and brought to the Curragh Hospital. Lieutenant Casey later died of his wounds.[19]

Jim Dunne was appointed OC of the Kildare Brigade column, which had a strength of sixty men, and with the brigade OC, Paddy Brennan, planned an attack on Rathangan barracks, which was held by about thirty-five National Army men:

> The building was hard to attack, as it had a canal, a river and a high wall at the back. P. Brennan opened the attack from behind a wall about 100 yards in front of the barracks. I took a party of ten men around to the back but could not get in a view of the barracks. After one hour I had to take my party around to the front of the barracks, and after consultation with P. Brennan I took charge of the riflemen. P. Brennan bombed the building, from cover of a low wall in front. He succeeded in putting nine bombs through the lower windows and driving the defenders to the top floor, where they came under our fire and were forced to surrender after the hours' fighting. We captured twenty-two rifles, twenty shotguns, seventy bombs and a large supply of ammunition. Ten Free State troops were wounded. We suffered no casualties. We could only use seven riflemen during the attack, as there was no room for more from the only position available. The Prosperous men attached to the column did guard duty around the town and did not take part in the actual attack. The attacking party was composed of men from Kill, Naas and Kilcullen. After the attack we went back to Coolcarrigan House, our headquarters. The garrison of Free State troops (forty) men at Robertstown retreated to Naas when we opened the attack on Rathangan.[20]

As fighting spread throughout the provinces casualties mounted. Commandant Seán Nolan of the National Army was killed in action on 5 July. Seán Nolan, 1st Eastern Division, and an IRA

Volunteer, George McDermott, were killed during a siege of a strongly fortified house at Curraghtown, near Trim, occupied by thirty-three republicans. Ironically, both men were twenty-four and both had served in the British army, in the Leinster Regiment, during the Great War, McDermott being wounded in action. The republicans had their headquarters at Curraghtown, in an unusual, large, unoccupied two-storey house. On the evening of 4 July, after a successful reconnaissance, an advance detachment of National Army troops from Navan, Trim and Kells crept up to the house. They called for reinforcements and 150 National Army troops arrived the next morning to take up positions. Meanwhile, the attacking party drove back the republican outposts, fatally wounding one republican soldier. As a new day dawned Commandant Seán Nolan dashed out into the avenue near the house to throw a bomb when a sniper shot him. The bullet passed through his lungs from left to right. A local priest anointed the wounded officer, who died soon after. A truce was called shortly after and the republican garrison surrendered.[21]

Seán Nolan, from Hospital Street, Kildare, was a very popular and prominent figure in Kildare town. He had served with distinction throughout the Great War and on his return took a major part in the work of the IRA. His body was brought back to his home town for burial. The remains were borne on the shoulders of members of the National Army, relieved by some of his old comrades-in-arms. The mournful dirge of the pipes of the Civic Guard band, playing 'Wrap the Green Flag Round Me', was heard as the sad procession wove its way to Grey Abbey Cemetery, followed by several hundred Civic Guards – resplendent in their new uniforms – units of National Army troops and mourning townspeople.[22]

On the same day that Seán Nolan died, in the southern part of the county near the Carlow border, IRA Volunteers Sylvester Sheppard and Laurence Sweeney were killed in action at Castledermot. Sheppard was from Kill Cottages, Monasterevin, while Sweeney was from Stillorgan, County Dublin, and a member of the Dublin Brigade. Republican troops had occupied Castledermot, and the following day soldiers from the National Army moved into the town. William Lawler, an eyewitness to the action, said:

> My brother Matty and I were playing that day in the old Franciscan Abbey, when I saw a Free State army armoured car coming down the street from the Dublin direction with a gun at the ready in its revolving turret. At the same time a lorry carrying opposing troops approached the town from the Baltinglass direction. Both vehicles came in sight of each other at Barry's Corner and I heard the rat-tat-tat of machine gun fire as the two sides joined battle. Before it ended a man in the lorry was dead. During the exchange of gunfire an ass in Mr Rice's field on the Carlow road was also killed.[23]

There was another clash at Carlow Gate, on the outskirts of the town, resulting in more casualties for the retreating IRA.[24] National Army troops now occupied the most southern extremity of the county.

In a vain attempt to stop the flames of Civil War spreading, the Labour Party called for a meeting of members of the Dáil at the Mansion House on 20 July. Only Labour members attended and the Provisional Government, rapidly gaining control of the country, made it clear that they intended to suppress the 'armed revolt' and would not compromise. That same day Michael Collins asked Acting Major-General Tobin to send a detail of troops to attend the Curragh races to see whether any of the 'Irregulars we want, attend. If there are any of them they could be put into the

Curragh Camp temporarily.' This was the reality of the Civil War: former friends and comrades were now spying on one another's old haunts.[25]

IRA veteran Ernie O'Malley was appointed to act as assistant chief of staff for the IRA and to organise the provinces of Leinster and Ulster. He moved to Tullow, County Carlow, where he arranged for attacks on Carlow town and Athy with the help of men from the Carlow Brigade.[26] After the capture of Rathangan, Paddy Brennan, brigade OC, and his vice-OC Jim Dunne decided to meet Ernie O'Malley at Bunclody, County Wexford, where he had his headquarters. They felt that, with reinforcements, Naas and the Curragh could be taken. They were also asking for permission to withdraw the 6th Battalion column from Baltinglass. O'Malley did not agree, informing them that he was falling back on Tipperary, and instructed Brennan and Dunne to bring all their men to Baltinglass. Dunne and Brennan returned to Coolcarrigan as National Army troops from the Curragh, Naas, Edenderry and Lucan converged on their headquarters at Coolcarrigan House. After the evacuation of Blessington, the only area in North Kildare which was then in the hands of the IRA was Coolcarrigan House, the residence of Lady Jane Wilson Wright, who was a cousin of Sir Henry Wilson, chief of the imperial staff, who was gunned down by the IRA in June. The house was garrisoned by about forty men from the 1st and 6th Battalions, many of the other republicans having left. They formed into defensive positions at Timahoe Cross to await the troops' advance.[27]

On the night of 10 July, while National Army troops in two columns were proceeding towards the republican stronghold, two men – Thomas Reilly, wearing his National Army uniform, and Paddy Tierney – approached the crossroads near the North-West Kildare Co-operative Society's stores. Seeing the National

Army uniform, IRA Volunteers from behind the fence adjoining the roadside opened fire. Thomas Reilly, a native of Oakwood, Valleymount, County Wicklow, was shot dead, a bullet entering through the lower part of his chest on the right side and emerging on the left side. Paddy Tierney, from Newbridge, was shot through both lungs, the bullet entering on the right side of his chest and passing out through the left. Reilly died at the scene, while Tierney was badly wounded.[28]

Tierney had joined the National Army, but had republican sympathies. He had called earlier to Mick Sheehan's in Newbridge where he asked if there were any IRA dispatches awaiting delivery. Sheehan told him to be in Coolcarrigan before dark as the IRA was expecting a National Army attack. Unknown to the republicans at Coolcarrigan, the two were coming to join them, but Tierney and Reilly were late and when they approached Timahoe Cross on Tierney's motorcycle they were shot. Tierney was brought to Naas Hospital and an armed guard placed outside his room. However, he was later spirited out the window of his room by sympathisers. The republicans retreated to Mr Curry's house on the south side of Prosperous and next day marched to Kilcullen, where a lorry was commandeered to take them to Baltinglass. They were pursued by National Army troops, who managed to take some prisoners.[29]

Kildare men were now operating in Baltinglass, Dunlavin and Tullow. Around thirty-five Kildare men joined the garrison in Baltinglass, bringing the total to seventy under the command of Commandant Byrne. Officer cadets from the Curragh attacked the barracks in Baltinglass but were beaten off. One section of Kildare men attacked an armoured vehicle carrying Commandant Tom Ennis, who was wounded. National Army reinforcements arrived and after five hours of fighting Baltinglass fell. Tom Derrig and Seán Lemass were with the garrison, but they escaped.[30] About twenty-five of the Kildare men fought their way out and returned home. On 4 August, superior forces captured over a dozen men of the Kildare flying column, including its commander, Jim Dunne, as they tried to blow up the railway bridge near Sallins.

A recruitment drive in July and August 1922 raised the numbers in the National Army to 60,000, vastly outnumbering the republican forces. By the middle of August the 'rebel south' had fallen. Republican resistance was half-hearted and neither side was very anxious for the fight. Naval landings by the National Army had outflanked strong republican positions in Cork and Kerry. Republican forces usually put up a token resistance in the towns and then faded into the countryside to employ the old tactics of guerrilla warfare, which had succeeded so well against the British. Meanwhile, Michael Collins went on a tour of the south to see how the army was progressing. Collins was concerned with the efficiency of the National Army, as only a minority of it was made up of experienced ex-IRA men he knew and could rely on. The ever-increasing National Army was largely made up of unemployed working-class youths and discharged Irish soldiers from the British army. Some of these had old scores to settle and others were in the army for what they could get out of it. Collins saw it as his responsibility to make them into a respectable National Army. Both republican and nationalist forces had plenty of new recruits, or 'trucers', who had not taken part in the war against the British. The influx of new recruits to both organisations led to a thinning of comradeship, which was responsible for much of the bloodshed.[31]

One of Collins' loyal allies was Peter Lawler of Halverstown, Naas. A veteran of the Great War, Peter had joined the Australian army and fought in the Pacific island campaign against the Germans and then with the 1st Australian Regiment (the famous Dinkums) in the Dardanelles. When he returned to Ireland in 1919, Lawler joined the Kildare Brigade IRA and was extremely proud of the fact that Michael Collins personally bestowed on him the insignia of rank as commandant in the National Army in 1922. Collins had a favour to ask – according to Frank Lawler, Peter's son – the assassination of Eamon de Valera, whose death he hoped might end the conflict. Commandant Lawler learned that de Valera had gone south and found him in County Carlow at the home of the late Kevin Barry. As an expert marksman, Lawler planned to shoot de Valera as he left the Barry home, but when word was sent to Collins he said no, it was too much to shoot his rival leaving the home of one of Ireland's greatest martyrs.[32] A few days later Collins was killed in an ambush as he toured the south. (Peter Lawler went on to become OC Cavalry Corps, Plunkett barracks, the Curragh, and later served in the Spanish Civil War as an officer with O'Duffy's Irish Brigade. He died on 22 August 1972.)[33]

On Saturday 12 August, Collins left Dublin for a tour of the south, passing through Naas where his Lancia touring car caught fire and only re-started with difficulty. The entourage continued on to their first official stop at Maryborough (Portlaoise). Collins' tour of inspection was called off when news of Arthur Griffith's death reached him in Tralee.[34] He returned to Dublin for the funeral. Arthur Griffith, whose father had worked as a compositor in Naas with the *Kildare Observer* before moving to Dublin, died of a cerebral haemorrhage, aged fifty, as he rose on the morning of 12 August.[35] Two days later, Michael Collins marched at the head of the funeral procession, resplendent in his new uniform of the commander-in-chief. 'I was at Arthur Griffith's funeral on 14 August', the author's great-aunt, Ellen Gaul, from Rathasker Road, Naas, recalled many years after the event. 'A week later I was in the same place at the funeral of Michael Collins.'[36]

At 6.15 on Sunday morning, 20 August, Michael Collins set

out from Portobello barracks in a convoy of vehicles to finish his tour of the south and 'to visit his old home place and his relatives and friends in West Cork', and, hopefully, to try to make peace. The convoy drove to Naas and stopped at the military barracks, where bugler Larry McGarr sounded the general salute. Its tones brought every member of the garrison to the barrack square, where General Collins shook hands with many of them and wished them well. The convoy then went on to Newbridge and then to the Curragh camp, where Collins carried out an inspection. The convoy continued on to Kildare and Monasterevin before making another stop, again in Maryborough, where Collins visited the prison.

Two days later Michael Collins was shot dead in an ambush at Béal na mBláth, just a few miles from his home. He was the only fatal casualty in the ambush. The nation mourned Collins' death and tributes poured in, even from his former enemies in Britain and Northern Ireland. In Kilmainham Gaol 1,000 republican prisoners knelt and said a decade of the rosary for the repose of his soul when they heard of his death. The chief of the general staff, General Richard Mulcahy, immediately ordered his men to remain calm and not to take reprisals. Bugler Larry McGarr from Naas was at the graveside of his commander-in-chief in Glasnevin Cemetery. He was certain he brought his old Fianna bugle with him but could not recall whether he sounded the bugle at the funeral.[37]

Father P. J. Doyle, parish priest of Naas from 1938 until his death in 1962, was an enthusiastic supporter and personal friend of Michael Collins:

> My last encounter with Collins was in Naas at the time he was on his tour of inspection of the Irish army posts. In his inspection he was ruthlessly intolerant of any defects, and hence these inspections raised the temperature of the army posts to a hectic degree. One day

I got a message from the commandant at Naas military barracks to go up at once, to function as a lightning conductor in the storm that was anticipated. After the inspection Collins came down to my house for a short time, and then left for Dublin. It was the last time I saw him alive.[38]

When the question arose, on his death, of bringing his body to Dublin, it was decided to have the body conveyed by sea to the North Wall, Dublin, owing to broken communications by road and rail. On the day the body was due to arrive, Father Doyle received a message from army headquarters and was taken by motor car to the North Wall in the company of General Richard Mulcahy and Gearóid O'Sullivan, where they met members of the government and a small group of Collins' most intimately devoted followers:

> There was a long and strained wait until about 2 o'clock, when we saw a light moving down the river. It was the boat from Cork, a cross channel liner. The boat's engines had been cut out, the spacious, empty decks were blazing with light, the solitary figure of the captain stood motionless on the bridge. In the inky darkness of the night the great, gleaming, white vessel came drifting towards us in eerie silence, like a phantom ship of destiny, borne on the black, swiftly in-flowing tidal waters of the Liffey.[39]

When the boat moored, Father Doyle accompanied the entourage on board and then walked in silence behind the coffin, mounted on a gun carriage, as it made its slow progress to City Hall. Here he sorrowfully took leave of the mortal remains of his great friend:

> It was in no excess of hollow sentimentality that I stooped, and with reverence and gratitude, kissed his forehead. On the morning of the

funeral Gearóid O'Sullivan told me that the army authorities had requested that I should officiate as deacon at the Requiem Mass, but the request had been refused by the Ecclesiastical authorities at the Pro-Cathedral, where the Requiem was celebrated. I walked in the funeral procession and stood beside the grave at Glasnevin Cemetery until the last sad rites were completed.[40]

7

GUERRILLA DAYS IN KILDARE

On 15 August 1922 about 250 republican troops under the command of Frank Aiken attacked Dundalk. Aiken, commanding the 4th Northern Division, the greater part of which was in Ulster, had tried to remain neutral during the Civil War, but Richard Mulcahy had sent men to Dundalk and captured Aiken's barracks through a breach of faith. Aiken and his officers were arrested and imprisoned in Dundalk Jail, but the jail wall was blown in by men under the command of John McCoy from South Armagh, and Aiken and several others escaped. On the day in question Aiken returned and captured the barracks, blowing up the lower portion of the building with mines. In fifteen minutes the well-timed operation resulted in the capture of the entire town and its garrison of 350 men. About 400 rifles, two eighteen-pounder guns and a huge amount of ammunition and stores were also captured.[1] Around 300 IRA prisoners, including about sixty from Kildare, were released and entertained to breakfast at the military barracks. Patrick O'Keefe, Kilcock, was one of the Kildare prisoners in Dundalk:

> On 14 August we were awakened by loud banging and shouting

(coming from outside) and cries of 'Get up boys, you are free'. We were not long dressing, there was noise and shouting outside our windows and then our cell doors opened. Frank Aiken and his men were after capturing the Free State military barracks and also the prison. We marched down to the military barracks, where we were supplied with guns to fight our way home. To me this was a day in a life-time, seeing over 200 IRA prisoners marching out and about the same amount of Free Staters marching in to take our place as prisoners ... When the arms in the barracks were divided, we went out of Dundalk in sections. We were about fifteen miles from Dundalk when we heard a loud explosion. One of our sections was after blowing up the railway bridge. That night we slept in a hay field.[2]

Patrick O'Keefe was recaptured after a running fight with National Army troops at Skreen, near Tara.

Jim Dunne and his captured column had been transferred to Dundalk Jail from Naas barracks and wanted to make their way back to the short-grass county so Dunne took command of sixty men from Kildare, who were armed with thirty rifles and some explosives. They met with another party of republicans and set out for Dunleer, County Louth, with instructions to blow up the railway bridge there, which was carried out by the battalion engineer, P. Magee. Dunne recorded what happened next:

Todd Andrews from Dublin HQ was in charge at Dunleer. He instructed me to cut across country for Kildare as best I could. Mick O'Neill of Celbridge, North Kildare Battalion, 1st Meath Brigade, had charge of another column of twenty men from that area and took another direction home. After travelling two days, mostly without food or sleep, we were surrounded by 500 Free State troops at Skreen,

County Meath. After a fight lasting from 6 p.m. to 10.30 p.m., I managed to break through the enemy ring with twenty men and rifles, and after travelling about five miles we put up at a farmhouse owned by two brothers named Duffy who lived near Fairyhouse race-course. We had our clothes dried, as it had rained all night and we were wet through. They also provided us with hot drinks and food. When we had got through the enemy ring, I had left a rearguard of ten men to hold back enemy troops. Those men were under the command of Patrick Magee, our engineer, an officer of Kill Company. Other men I can remember with him were Peter Mills, Kill, Jim Collins, Kilcullen, Jim O'Keefe, Kilcock. I can't remember the names of the others. Each man of the rearguard had been provided with 250 rounds of ammunition and was armed with a rifle. When they surrendered at 10.30 p.m. they had only seven rounds of ammunition left and the rifles were jammed and red hot. The Dublin Guards who had been attacking them had lost three men killed and several wounded.

The prisoners were lined up by the Dublin Guards to be shot, when the officer in charge of the Guards, Commandant Stapleton arrived on the scene. He congratulated our men on the fight they had put up and accorded them good treatment.

My column, after two days forced march, arrived back in Kill area, where we had to rest for a week. I got in touch with the Brigade OC, P. Brennan, and reformed the column. Several men who had come home with us from Dundalk were from Edenderry and Rhode areas in Offaly. I put E. Mitchell, from Castlejordan, in charge of six men, armed them with rifles and sent them home to their areas to carry on operations as a small column. E. Mitchell sent me monthly reports of all activities. I also sent rifles to Bracknagh, 5th Battalion area, and a column was formed under Jer Dooley. All rifles and dispatches were sent by canal boats to Miss Carroll, Cumann na mBan, who was a clerk in Murphy's Stores, Rathangan.

My column in Kill area in September 1922 consisted of about fifteen men. We had the co-operation of the Kilteel section of Kill Company, about nine men who had returned home after Baltinglass and who were armed.

My brigade took in Hollywood, Crehelp, Dunlavin, Ballitore, Ballyshannon, Kilcullen, the Curragh and Bracknagh and as far as Rhode, Edenderry, through Prosperous to Kill and the Dublin boundary. Our Brigade HQ was at Barnewall's, Lyons Cottage, Straffan, and all our dispatches went through the Misses Barnewall and Misses B. and Fanny O'Connor, Elm Hall, Celbridge. Misses May and Fanny Dunne, my sisters at Kill, and Miss Grehan, Naas, handled our dispatches and carried arms etc. for our men. Miss Peg Daly was the principal Cumann na mBan girl in Kildare town. Nearly all of these girls were afterwards interned.[3]

When he was released from Dundalk barracks, Jim Dunne befriended John McCoy of Armagh – the officer in charge of the attack on Dundalk – and later helped him escape from the Curragh camp. After the Civil War John McCoy moved to Dublin to work with the Military Pensions Board and in the 1940s moved to Kill, a few hundred yards from the Dunne home place at Greenhills.[4]

Whatever hope there had been of bringing the Civil War to a hasty end died with Michael Collins. Richard Mulcahy took over Collins' position as commander-in-chief of the National Army and his post as Minister for Defence. As both sides blamed each other for wrecking Ireland's future, Mulcahy demanded an unconditional surrender of the republicans, while control of the IRA slipped from Eamon de Valera to diehards like Liam Lynch, Ernie O'Malley and Tom Barry. Mulcahy and Collins had been the two outstanding leaders of the IRA during the War of Independence, but now Mulcahy faced his biggest test yet. History would show that

Mulcahy was the perfect man for the job – he was ruthless and did not tolerate failure.

The death of Collins also ensured that any attempt by republicans to coordinate a military campaign was weakened. The tendency now was to break up into smaller groups as the IRA was forced into more remote country districts. With the ending of the conventional fighting, the IRA returned to guerrilla warfare. Using tactics proven against the British, supply lines and communications were attacked. Republicans demolished bridges, trenched and blocked roads with fallen trees, and burned railway signal cabins. Post offices were raided, telephone communications destroyed and railways damaged. Patrols and search parties were in operation day and night. Movement between towns was hazardous. This angered the public, who wanted a return to peace, and the IRA began to lose support. Homes that were once opened to them were closed.

By the end of August de Valera could see that the republican cause in the field was lost. He had never had much heart in the fight anyway and he believed anger rather than idealism now continued the fight. The republican deputies did not attend the new Dáil, which met on 5 September with W. T. Cosgrave as president. The Cosgrave government was not only fighting a war, but also planning and putting into operation the country's administrative system. Local government was organised, a civil service set up and magistracy instituted.[5]

In September, Kildare IRA officer Paddy Brennan went to Dublin to take part in an attack on Oriel House, the headquarters of the Criminal Investigation Division (CID), situated on the corner of Westland Row. Oriel House was infamous as a 'knocking shop' where republican prisoners were ill-treated and tortured. A friendly CID man offered to help the IRA gain entry and access to CID files and guns. Michael Price, OC of the 1st Eastern Division, was in Dublin that night, along with Paddy Brennan as acting brigadier and Commandant Paddy Mannion. Brennan was to convey the captured arms back to his brigade at Kilteel. The plan went awry because a guard tried to draw a gun and was shot dead as the IRA entered the building. The IRA then retreated instead of continuing the attack. Commandant Mannion was wounded in a further exchange of fire at Mount Street Bridge. He was propped up against the bridge parapet and shot by National Army soldiers. (At his inquest a verdict of wilful murder was returned against the military.) Paddy Brennan was captured in the follow-up searches and Michael Price sent word to Jim Dunne to take charge of Kildare, and sent Lieutenant-Colonel Ted O'Kelly to help re-organise the county.[6]

Ambushes and general lawlessness continued in the county. A seventeen-year-old girl, Margaret Collins, a member of a republican family, was killed when she picked up a bomb hidden in a potato field at Grangemore, Brannockstown, on 18 September.[7] It was believed she had stumbled across a republican arms dump on her family's property.

On 3 October 1922, a government proclamation offered an amnesty to all of those in arms, provided they surrendered their arms on or before 15 October. The following day the Executive Council of the Free State Government decided to seek the support of the Catholic hierarchy in putting down the IRA. The bishops agreed to the government's request and, on 10 October, the Irish hierarchy in Maynooth issued a joint pastoral letter condemning the republicans and warning them that they would not be absolved in confession and would be denied the sacraments. The bishops supported the Provisional Government as the legitimate government and regarded armed opposition to it as a crime. With the passing of the deadline, military courts with powers to inflict the death penalty were set up. The pronouncement in the pastoral letter was strictly enforced by the majority of priests throughout the country and gave a cloak of moral authority to the Provisional Government in carrying out its executions. The republicans, understandably, viewed this with great bitterness, saying that the bishops had issued their opponents with a licence to kill.[8]

On 6 October about thirty republican prisoners escaped through a tunnel from the Curragh internment camp. Fifteen of them from the west and north of Ireland were brought to the Naas area for transportation back to their home counties. Commandant Jim Dunne brought a batch of ten men from the west to Celbridge. The safe house in which they were billeted was surrounded by National Army troops from Naas. Commandant Dunne and Tom Kealy of Celbridge held the troops off for an hour while the unarmed prisoners made their escape. Both Dunne and Kealy also escaped. Nine of the escapees were later recaptured after a ten-mile cross-country chase near the Kildare–Meath border.[9]

Raiding National Army troops from Naas arrested Dennis Hannon at a dance hall in Caragh on the night of 8 October. They continued on to Weld's public house where they found no wanted men and then proceeded to a house at Blackwood where they found Thomas Murphy, quartermaster 7th Brigade, with important documents and dispatches for republicans in the area. A week later, on 14 October, a car was ambushed at Louisa Bridge between Leixlip and Maynooth by Paddy Mullaney's column. Three shots were fired at the car and the passenger, Commandant Buggle, told the driver to stop and put out the lights. On getting out he was shot and wounded, and important National Army dispatches and his revolver were taken by the attackers, who numbered about twenty and were armed with rifles. Commandant Buggle was taken to Maynooth by the driver and then on to a Dublin hospital, where he recovered from his injuries.[10]

On 24 October, a small party of eight National Army troops was ambushed at Graney, about a mile from Castledermot. It was a well-planned and violent attack that showed the viciousness of the Civil War. Three soldiers died, one of whom was only sixteen. (While the legal age for enlistment was seventeen, many youths falsified their age – a practice which continued up until the 1960s.) The ambush took place at a sharp bend in the road, at a spot where four roads converged, known as Graney Cross. The attacking IRA party used a house nearby as their main position. For about an hour before the ambush occurred people passing along the roads in the locality were held up and ordered to take cover in some of the houses nearby. A number of men who were working on the roads in the area were also held up and taken to a place of safety. All the roads had been blocked by trees and the small group of soldiers were caught in a virtual deathtrap. The attackers outnumbered the National Army troops and they fired on the car using rifles, Lewis guns and revolvers.[11]

The National Army party was under the command of Lieutenant Edward Nolan and he gave this description of the ambush to the inquest the following day at the Carlow Workhouse:

> On Tuesday 24th October, I left Baltinglass about noon with Commandant Kenny, five men and the driver in a Crossley tender. We were going to Athy. Between Castledermot and Athy we ran short of petrol and the car stopped on the road. Commandant Kenny sent one of the men with dispatches to Athy on a bicycle, and a motor brought out petrol. We then proceeded to return to Baltinglass through Castledermot. We stopped at the Post Office for about five minutes, and then proceeded towards Baltinglass. When we came to Graney Cross and as we were passing by the cottage on the right side fire was opened upon the troops from the cottage. The first volley had

no effect. A second volley was fired quickly. The driver lost control of the car and it ran up on the ditch between ten and fifteen yards from the cottage. Fire was opened on all sides: from the cottage; a house at the cross; a low wall called the pound; and the old ruins to the left in the field. The second volley knocked out the whole party. Three men fell out of the car on to the road dead. The others were all wounded. I was wounded myself and dropped down flat on the road and crawled along the edge of the ditch, and when I got up, about seven yards in front of the cottage, I was covered by three men with revolvers. I was lying on my back in the ditch when I was ordered to put them up, and one man took the rifle and ammunition from me. I asked him to get me a drink of water in the house opposite. He promised to do so, but did not come back. About twenty men came out from the cottage and behind the ditch. They were all armed. I recognised amongst them three men … I cannot tell who fired the shots that killed the three men. After this they set fire to the lorry and then marched off in the direction of Knocknacree. Most of the firing was at close range and it was impossible to escape and the roads were barricaded. The car was standing still from the time it ran into the ditch and was bending over towards the road. The fire was opened up on us suddenly and without warning and we were not called on to surrender. I did the best I could for my wounded comrades with the assistance of neighbours. We were afterwards removed to Carlow. The firing came from revolvers, rifles and bombs. While the men were lying on the road the firing was kept up.[12]

Privates Edward Byrne, James Murphy and Patrick Allison were shot dead and fell out of the Crossley tender onto the road. Whilst on the road they were hit by more bullets. Private Edward Byrne, Bagnelstown, was hit four times and died from a wound above the heart. He was sixteen and had joined the National Army only three months previously. James Murphy, Kilkeegan, Baltinglass, had been in the National Army for ten months. He was forty and had been shot through the shoulder. Patrick Allison, Harristown, County Wicklow, was hit twice, in the head and stomach. He had seen service in France with the British army and been an active member of the IRA before the Truce.[13] The rest of the troops were wounded and, with the exception of Lieutenant Nolan, were all seriously injured. The IRA column burned the tender and took away all the arms except Commandant Kenny's revolver, which they probably overlooked. Mary Byrne, the mother of Edward, told the inquest:

> I have seen the body of Edward Byrne, now lying in the hospital of the Workhouse. He is aged sixteen years and had been in the National Army for three months. He is my son. I last saw him alive on Thursday last. I also identify the body of Patrick Allison.[14]

On the night of 14 October, a mine destroyed Killeen Bridge on the railway line between Sallins and Straffan, while a bridge outside Kildare was blown up four days later. The railway line was blocked for a considerable time.[15] In Newbridge indiscriminate shooting from the barracks in two separate incidents wounded a boy and a local man. On 3 November a party of eight men under a non-commissioned officer (NCO) were attacked from several points at Sallins railway station. Private Francis Crampton, Swordlestown, Naas, was killed and Private Whitt slightly wounded.[16] On the night of 25 November the IRA attacked Athy barracks with sustained rifle and grenade fire. The garrison replied using Lewis guns and rifles and the firefight continued for about half an hour. There were no casualties on either side. Desultory fire continued for another thirty minutes until the IRA left.[17]

Jim Dunne's column was particularly active around north-east Kildare and took part in:

> ... an attack on Free State troops at Sallins Station in which one Free State soldier was killed and two wounded. Several attacks took place on the main Dublin–Naas road. Two soldiers were killed and several wounded. One soldier was killed at Kill village when a convoy was attacked, and two more wounded.[18]

National Army casualties in Kildare, including three local men, for the latter part of the year were high:

> Pte Michael Bailey shot dead in ambush on Naas Road 19 October.
> Pte Peter Behan, Great Connell, Newbridge, killed in action on 22 October.
> Pte James Murray, killed in action in Castledermot on 24 November.
> Pte John Dooley, Loughbrown, Newbridge killed in an explosion in Wexford on 3 December.
> Cpl George McGlynn, Forge, New Row, Naas died of wounds on 4 December.[19]

In November, Commandant Patrick Mullaney planned to capture Baldonnel Aerodrome and bomb Beggar's Bush barracks and the Curragh military camp. Two IRA officers who were ex-British army airmen were to man two aeroplanes and drop bombs on Leinster House. About 100 men and 30 officers, including pilots, manned Baldonnel, a former British army air force base built in 1917, ten miles from Dublin. Paddy Mullaney had the cooperation of about thirty soldiers in the camp. Mullaney, a County Mayo-born national teacher from Leixlip, was OC of the North Kildare/Meath Brigade column. He had fought with the Kildare/Meath column during the War of Independence and was one of the Kildare leaders arrested at the beginning of the Civil War, along with Domhnall Ua Buachalla and Mick O'Neill. However, Mullaney had escaped on 20 August and linked up with his old comrades, assuming command of the Kildare/Meath column. (Ua Buachalla and O'Neill were sent to Dundalk, from where they also escaped.)[20]

Mullaney assembled his men in Celbridge for the operation. He was joined by Jim Dunne's column, Tom Harris with men from 4th Battalion (Prosperous) and W. Byrne, with the 6th Battalion column, bringing the number of republican troops to eighty. One hundred unarmed men were promised from the Dublin Brigade, but only twenty, under the command of IRA GHQ officer Todd Andrews, turned up. The purpose of these men being unarmed was to enable them to carry off the stores and equipment they expected to capture. Andrews called the operation off as he deemed there were not enough men to mount a successful attack. The columns returned to their areas and were called back again twice within two weeks. The Kildare men were fiercely enthusiastic about the attack – the first large-scale action of its kind planned by the anti-Treatyites. Jim Dunne said: 'The bombing of Leinster House might have ended the war.' He blamed Andrews for the failure. He said the Dublin men failed to rendezvous and that Andrews arrived with only seven men. On both occasions Dunne decided to call the operation off. Thirty men of the National Army garrison were ready to help, but the OC was adamant in his refusal to attack without the support of the Dublin Brigade, which made up more than half his strength. However, some of the guards at Baldonnel deserted to Mullaney's column.[21]

Mullaney's column continued on their mission to isolate Dublin by attacking bridges and communications in the North Kildare and

Meath area and launching ambushes on National Army troops, which resulted in six soldiers being wounded. The column was so successful in lifting rail tracks on the Great Western Railway line and burning signal boxes that a special Railway Protection Corps was formed to combat them. Post offices were also targeted in the area, yielding the column the means to survive. Mail cars going from Dublin were also easy pickings and the National Army was too hard-pressed to provide protection for them all. Mullaney challenged government forces at every opportunity and reported to his brigade OC: 'We intend to smash the railway and roads around the whole area and meet the Staters any time we get a crack at them with a fair chance.'[22]

On 1 December, Mullaney's column ambushed a ration lorry on its way to Maynooth, at Collinstown on the Leixlip to Maynooth road. The lorry had broken down and when the three occupants – Vice-Commandant Lynam, a quartermaster and a driver – got out they were fired on. Lynam and his two companions rushed for cover in the direction of the nearby canal bank. A Tommy gun fired on their shelter and the only means of escape was by way of the canal bridge – Pike's Bridge – further up the river. The republicans had also seen this, and seizing a motor car, rushed to the bridge. Commandant Lynam had no alternative but to surrender to the eighteen men who advanced towards him, though his driver had managed to slip away. The two National Army soldiers were disarmed and taken prisoner and brought to Grangewilliam House, the residence of Mr Kiely, which had been occupied by the republicans and was close to the road. News of the lorry, which had been left burning on the road, reached a National Army unit searching trains near Maynooth and they contacted troops at Maynooth, Trim, Naas, Lucan and Portobello barracks. Seven officers and forty men from the barracks, with a Whippet armoured car, a Fiat and five tenders, set out for Collinstown and were reinforced at Pike's Bridge by a tender from Naas.

At Pike's Bridge the IRA opened fire on the lead vehicles and one man in the second vehicle was wounded. The IRA had taken up positions in an old churchyard and some woods south of the road and canal. The National Army troops dismounted and returned fire, forcing the republicans to evacuate the churchyard. A party of troops under Brigadier McDonnell went round the right flank via Collinstown House while another party, under Commandant Saurin and Captain Trayner, with the Whippet, crossed Pike's Bridge under fire. The IRA at Pike's Bridge commenced a running fight across country, closely followed by National Army troops, with the armoured car moving along the road covering the advance of the troops with machine-gun fire. They set out for Grangewilliam House and in extended formation advanced on the republicans' position. There was little cover and they were exposed much of the time.

Two National Army soldiers became separated from the main group. While crawling forward, Private Joseph Moran and his comrade were observed and fire was opened on them from republicans in the house. Private Moran was shot through the head and died within seconds. His companion, still under fire, crept over to him. 'He never spoke a word, but just lay quite still on his back,' he later told a reporter. Some of his attackers came out of the house and woods surrounding the house on the left and called on him to surrender. The National Army soldier was disarmed and taken prisoner. Private Moran's weapon and equipment were also retrieved. A native of Naas, he lived with his wife at Harbour View, Kilcock.

The National Army troops advanced and the IRA used a Tommy gun and a Lewis gun to repel the attackers for over an hour as National Army reinforcements arrived from outlying areas. Eventually fire from the National Army was so intense that Commandant Mullaney gave the order to evacuate and they left, taking three prisoners with them. However, as the republicans retreated under steady fire they abandoned their prisoners. An armoured car and a Crossley tender patrolled the roads and a large body of National Army soldiers moved along the road, via Ballygoran House near to Kilwogan, and surrounded the IRA column. At around four o'clock Commandant Saurin and Captain Trayner's group came across the IRA column near Ballygoran on the Kildare–Meath border. Three of the column men were wearing Free State uniforms. They spotted the National Army troops and opened fire, but quickly realising their position was hopeless, surrendered after about ten minutes. The running fight had lasted about four hours.

Twenty-two republicans, three of them badly wounded, were captured, complete with their arms: one Tommy gun, one Lewis machine gun, twenty-one rifles, one Mauser 'Peter the Painter' automatic pistol, five revolvers, five bombs and over 1,000 rounds of assorted ammunition. All the captured prisoners were initially taken to Kilmainham Gaol, where five were recognised and identified as deserters from the National Army: former Corporals Leo Dowling and Sylvester Heaney, and former Privates Tony O'Reilly, Terence Brady and Lawrence Sheehy.[23] They had deserted from their posts at Baldonnel Aerodrome several days earlier with their arms and joined Mullaney's column. The five ex-soldiers were tried by court martial at Kilmainham on 11 December on the charges of:

> Treachery on the 1st December 1922 in that they at Leixlip assisted certain armed persons in using force against the National troops.

> Treacherously communicating and consorting with the armed persons mentioned in the first charge, in the place and at the time mentioned.[24]

They were convicted and all five were executed by firing squad on 8 January 1923 in Portobello barracks – although some reports say the executions occurred in Keogh (formerly Richmond) barracks. Leo Dowling was born at Carna, the Curragh; Tony O'Reilly was born at Simonstown, Celbridge; Sylvester Heaney was from Dunleer, County Louth; Lawrence Sheehy was from Braystown, County Meath; and Terence Brady was from Wilkinstown, Navan, County Meath.

The capture of Mullaney's column was a big blow to the IRA in the area. They had been responsible for four attacks on National Army troops and for the cutting of telephone and telegraph wires, raids on mails, post offices and canal barges, and the destruction of six signal cabins and two bridges.[25]

On the night before his execution Leo Dowling wrote to his parents from his cell in Kilmainham:

> I hope this letter won't make you unhappy. Well we must always take things as they come as whatever is the will of God will be done. Anyhow though 'tis a good thing to be happy in this world 'tis better to be happy in the next. This world is really only a valley of tears – so you must not fret when you read this letter.
>
> My dear Mother you know a little of the charge against me. Well after about one month my sentence has come & though 'tis the extreme penalty 'tis all for the best. Thank God I'll have the priest now in short, & don't fret for I'll be prepared to go in the morning.
>
> Two officers brought in the sentence this evening, they were rather nice fellows. They seemed sorry to be the bearers of such news. Please

God I'll be able to walk out tomorrow without flinching. I admit it appears a hard thing but it's the end and I like to die a soldier. It is not the same as being shot down fighting but one has the consolation of seeing the priest beforehand.

Of course I was expecting this but I did not like to tell you. All I ask is your prayers and don't fret about me. I'll be all right with God's help.

I will close now asking God to bless, protect & strengthen you, my own dear mother and father.

Your loving son,

Leo xxxx[26]

The remainder of the column was brought to Mountjoy Jail to be tried by a military tribunal. Since the men of the column were captured under arms they faced the death penalty and after much agonising, debate and consultation, Mullaney as commanding officer authorised his men to sign an undertaking which went as follows:

> I promise that I will not use arms against the parliament elected by the Irish people or the government for the time being responsible to that parliament, and that I will not support in any way such action. Nor will I interfere with the property of others …

Shortly after the removal to Mountjoy, eight of the Leixlip column signed. Mullaney and four others, however, held out. In mid-March 1923 these five were informed they were due for trial by military court at the end of the month. Trial would inevitably mean the death sentence. Finally, Mullaney authorised the remaining men to sign the undertaking and did so himself. Paddy Mullaney was sentenced to four years' imprisonment.[27] As a sentenced prisoner he was one of the last released on 7 June 1924 as part of a general amnesty. Mullaney was later dismissed from his teaching post as a result of his activities as a republican. However, parents and pupils supported him, and there was a school strike in Leixlip. He was later reinstated, but returned to his native Balla, County Mayo, where he was prominent in Gaelic Athletic Association (GAA) affairs.[28]

The takeover of Kildare RIC barracks, April 1922. *(Photo: Local Studies, Genealogy and Archives Department, Newbridge Library)*

Above: Lieutenant John Wogan Browne shot dead in Kildare during a payroll robbery in February 1922. *(Photo: John Wogan Browne)*

Right: Annie Moore, Rathbride, whose brother and fiancé were executed in December 1922. *(Photo: John O'Reilly)*

The cottage at Mooresbridge where the Rathbride column were captured in December 1922. *(Author's collection)*

Newbridge barracks, which was used as an internment camp during the Civil War. *(Photo: Local Studies, Genealogy and Archives Department, Newbridge Library)*

Rathbride column Volunteers. *Clockwise from top left:* Thomas Behan, Stephen White, Patrick Mangan, James O'Connor, Patrick Nolan and Jackie Johnston. *(Author's collection)*

Below: The coffins of the seven men executed at the Curragh rest in Kildare courthouse before reinterment at Grey Abbey graveyard 1924. *(Photo: Local Studies, Genealogy and Archives Department, Newbridge Library)*

Hare Park internment camp, the Curragh, *c.* 1914. *(Photo: Local Studies, Genealogy and Archives Department, Newbridge Library)*

Art O'Connor of Celbridge, Kildare TD who took the anti-Treaty side and was captured in the Dublin city centre fighting. *(Photo: Dan O'Connor)*

Joseph Bergin, murdered by National Army officers at Milltown, December 1923. *(Photo: Local Studies, Genealogy and Archives Department, Newbridge Library)*

Kildare barracks, former British artillery barracks, which became a Civic Guard depot. *(Photo: Local Studies, Genealogy and Archives Department, Newbridge Library)*

Palmerstown House, home of Lord Mayo, burned down in January 1923 by the IRA. *(Photo: Local Studies, Genealogy and Archives Department, Newbridge Library)*

Above left: Jim Dunne of Kill, OC Kildare Brigade IRA. *(Photo: Brian Dunne)*

Above right: Jimmy Whyte, Naas Company IRA, who escaped from Newbridge camp in 1922. *(Photo: James Pogge)*

Left: Francis Brennan, a member of the Mullaney flying column captured in December 1922. *(Photo: Christopher Lee)*

Newbridge Fife and Drum Band, St Patrick's Day, 1922. Among the band were men and boys who took both sides in the Civil War. *(Photo: Local Studies, Genealogy and Archives Department, Newbridge Library)*

New Civic Guard barracks, Station Road, Newbridge, *c.* 1923. *(Photo: Local Studies, Genealogy and Archives Department, Newbridge Library)*

Michael and Jim Sheehan, Newbridge, *c.* 1922. They took the anti-Treaty side, while their uncle joined the National Army. *(Photo: Local Studies, Genealogy and Archives Department, Newbridge Library)*

Below: Pipers lead the National Army contingent at the handover of Beggar's Bush barracks. *(Author's collection)*

8

THE GREAT ESCAPE

In August 1922 an internment camp with housing for about 1,200 republican prisoners was opened in the former British army cavalry barracks in Newbridge, which became the central detention centre for the twenty-six counties after the outbreak of the Civil War. In October 1922, 112 prisoners escaped, in the largest prison break in Irish penal history. The plan was designed and carried through by certain of the prisoners' leaders who had served long apprenticeships in prison under the British regime, and a remarkable feature of the escape was that it constituted the longest subterranean effort ever made by Irish prisoners seeking liberty. A further notable feature was that a large number of prisoners broke out the first night and their absence was successfully covered up the next day, with a further batch of prisoners escaping the following night. The achievement was all the more remarkable when it is considered that the prison authorities had adopted the usual precaution of placing spies amongst the prisoners so that inside information might be available to them.[1]

Thomas McMahon was OC of the republican prisoners in Newbridge camp. Among the internees from County Kildare were: Jim Collins, Maurice Lambe, Jim Mackey, Harry Myers,

Charlie and Hugh Curran, Kilcullen; Seán Hayden, Athy; Tom Harris, Prosperous; W. Byrne, Ballysax; Frank Bourke, Carbury; Seán Tracey, Naas; Kit Lynam, Pat and Jim O'Keefe, Kilcock; and Bertie Graham and Bill 'Squires' Gannon, Kildare. Newbridge barracks was a former British army artillery and cavalry barracks, which housed 800 men and around 500 horses. The IRA prisoners were housed in the 'Cupola' building in the centre of the barracks, which had a very large recreation area, including a hockey pitch, on the east side. This hockey pitch was converted to a Gaelic football pitch and some guards and internees recalled that the fine football matches played in Newbridge barracks were their strongest memory of the Civil War. Kildare defeated Dublin in the internee's Leinster final by 3–6 to 1–5 in October 1922. Among those playing for Kildare that day was Bill Gannon, who as captain of Kildare in 1928 was the first man to lift the Sam Maguire cup when Kildare won their fourth All-Ireland. When Maddenstown played Kildare in Newbridge the following February, noise from the spectators was drowned out by the cheers from inside the barracks, where an internees' match was taking place.[2]

By October there were about 1,500 prisoners in Newbridge barracks, many having arrived from the prison ship *Arvonia*, which was at anchor a few miles off Dun Laoghaire harbour. Over 700 prisoners were confined in half the steerage portion of the vessel. Food was short, with only one meal per day, consisting of a small amount of tea and dry bread. Sanitation was virtually non-existent. Prisoners slept where they could and the experience was not easily erased from the memory of those who lived through it. Danger of an epidemic necessitated a transfer – some of the prisoners going to Gormanstown and the rest to Newbridge – and in both cases the change was welcome. The diet in Newbridge left much to be desired, but there was at least an absence of the ship rolling and tossing, the luxury of a good wash and a bed to lie upon.[3] Brothers Pat and Jim O'Keefe, Kilcock, were on board the *Arvonia*:

> When we arrived it was full of prisoners from Cork, Limerick and Kerry. When we got on board there was hardly any room – it was like Hell on earth – on top and bottom decks. Jim and myself stayed on the top deck, to go below you would be suffocated with stench and foul air.
>
> We had to sleep where we were standing, some got under the seats to sleep only to find that all the urine went down a channel underneath. We were like a lot of 'wicked dogs'. Bread was fired in, the best catcher getting the most. In a short time most of the prisoners got the itch or scabies. A doctor came on board and ordered their transfer to the mainland. Jim scratched his arms, went to the doctor and was put on the transfer list.
>
> On the day the relief ship came all the sick were put on board. I was very depressed over parting with Jim. Then the officer-in-charge said, 'There is room for two or three more. Who will volunteer to come?' I accepted immediately, along with Kit Lynam. I was glad to get off the ship. Jim told me that on a few days previous they were thinking of scuttling her with all on board. Also on the prison ship was the bulletproof car which Michael Collins had the day he was shot. It was brought by sea from Cork to Dublin.
>
> The relief ship sailed over to the North wall, where we disembarked and went by rail to Newbridge Detention Camp (or Barracks). The rooms were big, holding about ten or twelve prisoners. The ground outside was quite large, having plenty of room to move around. A lot of the leaders were interned there. Tom Harris, TD, was their recognised leader, and I was in the same room as him. An escape plan got under way, to tunnel from the room to the sewer. It took a few weeks to complete, from the old Barrack into the sewer and then

under the field to the Liffey. The night of the escape, Tom Harris allowed Jim O'Keefe and Kit Lynam to come with me. We went on the third batch and got free.[4]

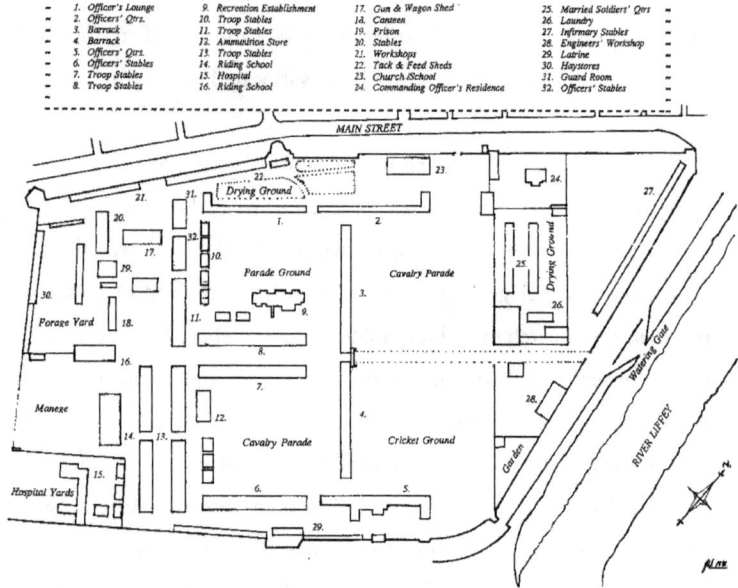

Plan of Newbridge Barracks 1908.
During the Civil War Barracks 3 and 4 and the stables housed Republican prisoners.

Map of the Newbridge barracks, former British cavalry barracks, which became a major internment camp (Paul Cooke)

It was not long until the active minds amongst the leaders were busy with plans of escape. Many plans were discussed and rejected.[5] The original idea was to dig three tunnels to free all prisoners, but this was thought to be too ambitious.[6] The veteran escape artists soon noticed that the sewer traps ran in a line across the quadrangle by the married quarters in the direction of the River Liffey, which flowed near the barracks. Thus, argued some of the conspirators, there must be an outlet for the river. Therefore, if they got to the sewer there was a good chance of escape. Others objected that the end of the sewer would be underwater, but this was countered by the argument that an exit could be made earlier, and an old building on the bank of the Liffey in a direct line with the sewer traps was pointed to as likely to afford cover. Of course, the possibility of escape by this means might have been foreseen and precautions taken by the prison authorities, but it was decided to take the gamble in the absence of a better plan. The 'Cupola' block was about 500 yards from the river, so the magnitude of the task undertaken can easily be understood.

The group on the ground floor of a block near the tower made a start. Direct descent into the sewer was not possible and it was found that a tunnel of approximately thirty feet in length needed to be cut to connect with the sewer. The line of the sewer near the buildings could only be guessed at. Nothing daunted the chosen few who commenced the formidable task. With a saw manufactured from a dinner knife, a square of flooring was cut from beneath one of the trestle beds. Carefully trimmed and with the marks of cutting erased, the square fitted into place and defied detection. With a pointed poker for a pick and a fire shovel to dig with, the work was quickly under way, a careful watch being kept on the movements of the guards. Day after day progress was made, with many narrow escapes from discovery as, frequently, some of the guards were in the room, whilst the 'miners' were at work beneath the floor.[7] Originally, soil from the tunnel was disposed of beneath the floor of the room, but later, the loose earth was stored in the top floor of a three-storey building in the camp and remained undiscovered until the demolition of the barracks in the 1960s when it was thought to be peat from the Bord na Móna factory, which occupied part of the barracks site from 1939–40.[8]

The day came when the sewer was located and penetrated, but the escapees' troubles were far from over. The sewer had been out of use for some time and though it was possible to stand upright and walk through, the air was so foul that it was impossible to explore for about a week. One brave adventurer who entered the sewer was violently ill for some days. Then there arose the difficulty of finding the correct route in a network of sewers. One of the explorers was lost for the best part of a day in his attempt to find his way back. Problem after problem was overcome in the most astounding way. Not only was the correct route discovered, but deep in the earth, 500 yards from the only exit, a way out was cut from the sewer, through the floor of a sawmill building on the banks of the Liffey. Republican prisoners have been notable for many incredible feats in the pursuit of liberty, but none more remarkable for tenacity of purpose and determination to succeed than the achievement of the men who opened the way for the escapees from Newbridge.[9] An exit was made in the centre of the sawmill and carpenter's workshop near the Liffey bridge, erected on a green space between the roadway and the river. The exit was tunnelled underneath a wheel seating in the sawmill, which connected with the sewer.[10]

It was decided to free prisoners from outside the area first and local men would leave the camp last.[11] On the fine night of Saturday 14 October there was a swift exodus and about thirty prisoners made a successful escape.[12] The following day was one of high tension as those involved endeavoured to cover the absence of their comrades. Many inquiries were made for prisoners who were absent and towards evening it was obvious that vague suspicions were aroused. With the coming of nightfall it was decided to rush another batch for freedom and at this time a search party of military actually entered the square. Soon a further group of prisoners were on the way to liberty.

An untitled account in the *Leinster Leader* some years after the event described the actual escape:

The lifting of the flooring revealed a dark pit into which one dropped. 'Feet first,' a voice whispered and guided one's foot to a hole in the side of the pit. Feet first and face upwards a prisoner wriggled along until his feet found an opening in the floor of the tunnel. 'Drop your feet and turn them backwards,' whispered the same voice, and one found that the feet rested in about twelve inches of water, and having successfully wriggled the rest of the body through, found that further progress had to be made on hands and knees and that broken bottles, tins, and other junk did not tend to make the journey easier. Holding the heel of the man in front and similarly held by the man following progress was made slowly in the pitch darkness. The quiet noise of the flowing water and the heavy breathing of the men broke the silence, which was enjoined on all, save when some unlucky one made unexpected contact with some sharp obstacle.

'Talk about Lough Derg,' muttered a disgruntled voice in the rear, and a titter of laughter was sharply suppressed. The escapees pressed on. 'Pass back word for silence. Passing under the grating,' came from in front and was duly passed on. At last came an order, 'Up here,' and one found the ground rising and the water was left behind. 'Through here,' and still a further opening – this time through a floor. Then quickly came the orders: 'You are in the house on the bank of the river. There is an armed guard on the bridge. When the door is opened don't walk, but roll down the slope to the river and across. Don't make noise or you'll be under machine gun fire. Good luck. Make your way as best you can.' The door was opened. The lights from the bridge shone faintly on the river, outlining a fleeting glimpse of figures moving about there. Behind, the barracks was outlined in electric lights. The escapees rolled quickly down the slope and into the cold water. No one spoke. To be caught in the river would be fatal. They reached the opposite bank at last. Quickly way was made up the slope to a barbed wire fence which was quickly crossed. From there the escapees were in open country.[13]

Emergence from the tunnel was a simple matter as the prisoners were concealed from the view of the sentries and the lookout posts erected high over the corners of the barrack wall. On coming up in the shed the prisoners left the sawmill by the back door leading to the river. Just after midnight the sentries noticed forms moving in the vicinity and opened fire. It was thought at least one man was wounded.[14] On the escape being detected the shed was surrounded, and a number of prisoners who were on the point of leaving, or were still in the sewer, were recaptured.[15] When the discovery was made, the alarm and the firing kept the inhabitants of the town in a state of panic for some time. Among the men who got safely away were: Tom Harris, former Kildare Brigade OC; William Byrne, Ballysax, OC 6th Battalion; T. J. Williams, Jimmy Whyte and Captain Jack Rafferty, Naas; Patrick and Jim O'Keefe from Kilcock; Kit Lynam; and a large number of Kildare men, all of whom reported back for duty.[16] Tom Harris asked Divisional OC Michael Price for his command back and resumed duty as the brigade OC.[17]

T. J. Williams, Naas, escaped from Newbridge in the second batch. He had also been on board the *Arvonia* prison ship.[18] Jack Rafferty and Jimmy Whyte had previously escaped from Dundalk Jail. After the split Jimmy Whyte had taken the anti-Treaty side and served with the Kildare column during the Civil War until his capture. His former commandant, Jim Dunne, said, 'There wasn't a better or braver man.'[19] His future brother-in-law, Jack Cassidy, formerly of the combined Meath/Kildare column, was in the

National Army and was one of the cycling troops from Meath who captured Jimmy in 1922. Most of the time they tipped each other off to raids, as Jack was dating Jimmy's younger sister Mary at the time. Jimmy Whyte was imprisoned in Newbridge and, according to relatives, 'he always said he didn't stay too long'.[20]

Mick Sheehan was one of the local prisoners awaiting his turn to escape:

> There was terrible shooting heard all over the town on the night and the army carried out raids on houses of the families of their captives, Sheehan's household included. With absolutely no regard for men, women or children alike, the soldiers terrified parents, lying that all attempted escapees had been shot in the river. On the same night, John [Sheehan] and Bridget's son, Joe, ten years old, was pulled from his bed where he lay ill at the time. His mother later got Father Horan, the curate in Newbridge, to call to the barracks inquiring if her other son, Mick, was one of those shot, or if he were still alive.[21]

A large force of National Army troops from Naas, Newbridge and the Curragh combed the area after the breakout. One escaped prisoner and William Clifford, an active republican from Kilcullen, were picked up in sweeps in the Harristown area on 1 November. Three escapees were picked up in Caragh the following day – two were Dubliners, while the other was from Enniscorthy. On their arrest two were found to be armed; one had a revolver and the other a Lee Enfield rifle.[22] The total number of prisoners who left by the tunnel was 149, of whom 37 were recaptured, 112 gaining their freedom.[23]

Despite the 'Great Escape', Newbridge camp remained home to hundreds of republicans for the next two years. Dubliner C. S. 'Todd' Andrews arrived in Newbridge internment camp in the summer of 1923 and remained there until April 1924 when he was finally released:

> It was an enormous place with wide parade grounds, many stables with saddle rooms attached, a spacious sports field, a hospital, kitchens and canteens. The extensive barrack blocks were three storeys high. The Free State authorities had converted the complex into the largest internment camp in the country and it already held nearly two and a half thousand prisoners. On arrival we were looked over by the Camp Governor and his staff. It did not take long to realise that their attitude to us was very different from the humane behaviour of their counterparts in Cork Female Jail. As we were 'processed' into internment, we found them to be a brusque, bullying lot.
>
> We were allocated a number and a billet before being let loose into the compound. My number was 2571 and I was assigned a billet in one of the barrack blocks. We were immediately surrounded by friends – mine being, of course, Dubliners – who assured us that it was unnecessary to pay any attention to the billet allocation. Some very old friends of mine whisked me off to share their quarters, army hut number 60, which housed about thirty Dublin men mainly from the Four Courts garrison … By the time I had been fed and settled in I knew that relations between the prisoners and the Camp authorities were very bad. A few weeks earlier following the discovery of a tunnel some of the prisoners had been beaten by the guard and others, caught more or less in the act of escape, had been taken to the 'glasshouse' in the Curragh where they were roughly treated before being returned to Newbridge. Parcels and letters were stopped though they had been resumed just before we arrived. The prisoners had been given a bad time by parties of Staters who raided their huts or dormitories, upsetting the furniture and scattering their belongings. It was the kind of upheaval that invariably occurs

in internment camps when escapes, whether successful or otherwise, are attempted.[24]

With effect from 6 December 1922 the Provisional Government ceased to exist and the Irish Free State came into being. The Speaker opened the first meeting of the Free State parliament at Leinster House by administering the oath to the Dáil deputies. William Cosgrave was elected president of the Executive Council without opposition. Keeping the Finance Ministry for himself, Cosgrave nominated an Executive Council composed of Kevin O'Higgins as vice-president, Richard Mulcahy, Eoin MacNeill, Ernest Blythe, Joe McGrath and Desmond Fitzgerald, with each minister retaining the office he had held in the Provisional Government. Having approved the nominations the Dáil agreed to establish a committee which would appoint external ministers for agriculture, fisheries and the post office. Sixty senators were also elected.[25]

No sooner had the Free State come into existence than the Dáil and the country were shocked by a new kind of outrage and by the government's reaction. On 7 December Seán Hales, TD, was shot dead as he left the Ormond Hotel on his way to the Dáil. His companion, Pádraic Ó Máille, deputy speaker, was seriously wounded. Both men had voted for the Special Powers Bill. In an emergency meeting Mulcahy submitted the Army Council's proposal for the immediate execution of four imprisoned IRA leaders: Rory O'Connor, Liam Mellows, Dick Barrett and Joe McKelvey. On the following morning, the four were executed in Mountjoy Jail. A proclamation dated 8 December announced the existence of an assassination conspiracy and extended the military's power of summary execution.[26]

One of the great blots on pro-Treaty conduct, and a serious blow to republican morale, was the campaign of executions. Under martial law during the War of Independence, British military courts had imposed sentences of death by hanging, death by shooting, penal servitude for between three years and life, and imprisonment for up to two years. There were twenty-four executions for political offences carried out in 1920–21.[27] The military courts of the Provisional Government had a conviction rate of 85 per cent in cases in which a finding of 'waging war' was reached. A wide variety of sentencing options were made use of. Death sentences were imposed and confirmed in 29 per cent of cases tried. Seventy-seven executions were carried out between December 1922 and April 1923, compared with the twenty-four executions by the British.[28] In December 1922 the executions in the Curragh camp was the largest single group of executions conducted between 1919 and 1923.

9

'SEVEN OF MINE,' SAID IRELAND

Three episodes of the Civil War are vital factors in the memory of that most bitter struggle. They are the death of Michael Collins, the atrocities in Kerry and the executions – these evoke the most bitterness. Thirty-seven republicans were executed from 1919–21, while, in the period from December 1922 to June 1923, the Free State authorities executed seventy-seven republicans. A month after the passing of the Emergency Regulations, four young men were brought out at dawn and executed. They had been caught in Dublin with loaded revolvers, preparing a street ambush. A month later, when Dáil Deputy Seán Hales was shot dead in a street ambush, the Free State Government acted swiftly and ruthlessly: Rory O'Connor, Liam Mellows, Joseph McKelvey and Richard Barrett, all of whom had been in prison since the surrender of the Four Courts, were executed in Mountjoy Jail. These men, one from each of the four provinces, were among the finest of their remarkable generation. It was an immoral and illegal act and that same month, December 1922, a similar act was applied in County Kildare with the same ruthlessness.

Seven men were executed in the Glasshouse, in the Curragh

camp on 19 December in the biggest official execution of the Civil War. They were Patrick Bagnall and Patrick Mangan, Fairgreen, Kildare; Joseph 'Jackie' Johnston, Station Road, Kildare; Bryan Moore and Patrick Nolan, Rathbride, Kildare; Stephen White, Abbey Street, Kildare; and James O'Connor, Bansha, County Tipperary. These seven men, along with Commandant Thomas Behan, Rathangan, all members of the Rathbride column, were found in a dugout at Mooresbridge, on the edge of the Curragh, on the night of 13 December. Armed with rifles bought from a soldier stationed in Naas barracks, they were under the command of Commandant Bryan Moore, a veteran IRA officer, and comprised a section of the 6th Battalion column.[1]

Mass card for Tom Behan, Rathangan, killed by National Army troops in December 1922. (Author's collection)

Flying columns were created by the IRA during the War of Independence from men 'on the run', i.e. those who had to leave their homes, for fear of arrest, or of being murdered, by the British forces. During the Civil War the anti-Treaty IRA unit operating in the Kildare–Curragh area was known by the Free State authorities as the Rathbride column. As well as the eight men just mentioned it consisted of Joseph Kelly, Rathangan; Pat Moore (brother of Bryan), Rathbride; and Jimmy White (brother of Stephen). Four of the men – Mangan, Nolan, Johnston and O'Connor – were local railway workers.[2]

Thomas McEvoy from Dublin had taken the anti-Treaty side in the Civil War and was transferred from the 5th Dublin Battalion to district headquarters. There he served as a brigade engineer in Dublin, Louth and Kildare, where his commanding officer was Tom Harris. He took part in the blowing up of the Liffey Bridge in Celbridge in October 1922, and the burning of a Liffey junction signal cabin. On 2 November 1922, McEvoy was arrested in The Downings, Prosperous, County Kildare, and was imprisoned in Newbridge internment camp until Christmas week 1923. He makes a poignant reference to the seven members of the Rathbride column executed in the Curragh in December 1922, as well as their intelligence officer, Tom Behan, who was shot dead in dubious circumstances, saying that: 'Seven of my comrades were executed. The Brigade I/O [Intelligence Officer] was murdered. I was Brigade Engineer.' This suggests that Thomas McEvoy had also been involved with the Rathbride column, which was responsible for the destruction of bridges and the derailing of trains in the Kildare area before their capture at Mooresbridge in December, a month after McEvoy's arrest.[3]

The Rathbride column operated close to Kildare town. In October, the group had sent a runaway engine down the main

Kildare line. A railway bridge near Kildare was blown up and an engine and some wagons, from which the driver and fireman had been forcibly removed, were sent crashing into it. To the authorities it was obvious that some of the men engaged were railway workers, because of their knowledge of train driving. Five of them had apparently taken part in an attempt to disrupt communications by derailing train engines on 11 December, when two engines were taken from a shed at Kildare and sent down the line towards Cherryville. One engine ran out of steam and did no harm, while the other overturned and blocked the line for some time. (The Cherryville junction was vitally important as it had railway links to the west and south.) A third engine was also taken out at Kildare and driven into the turntable pit at the station; in addition, a wagon of coal was also crashed into the pit.[4] On another occasion the column ambushed a party of troops at the Curragh siding, wounding two, and a policeman was accidentally shot dead by the troops returning fire. It was also alleged that goods trains had been looted and shops robbed in the locality, a claim refuted by the supporters and families of the men. The *Kildare Observer* reported on raids in November 1922 by a number of armed men in motor cars, on tobacconists, pubs, the Railway hotel and a provision merchant. Some of the Rathbride column were positively identified by eyewitnesses.[5]

On 10 October, a proclamation by the Free State Government announced that anyone who fought against, was found under arms, or committed an act of war against the government would face the death penalty.[6] On 13 December a detachment of National Army troops from the Curragh raided a farmhouse at Mooresbridge, about one-and-a-half miles from the Curragh camp. They 'found the proprietress in possession of a fully loaded Webley revolver'. Some reports say the troops went away and came back some time later. The soldiers searched the farmhouse, where one or two men and Annie Moore – daughter of the owner, not the proprietress as claimed in the official report – were arrested. They then went into the stables across from the front entrance of the farmhouse. One of the soldiers banged his rifle butt against the floor and heard a hollow sound. They found an entrance to a 'dugout' and threatened to throw grenades in unless the occupants surrendered. As the occupants had no other way out they had no option but to capitulate. Annie Moore's son, John O'Reilly, claims the dugout was in fact an unfinished tunnel, which was to lead out to the nearby railway line.[7]

In total ten men and Annie Moore were arrested and the dugout yielded ten rifles, 200 rounds of ammunition, four bombs, two grenades, an exploder, a roll of cable and food supplies. The soldiers assaulted several of the detainees – Annie Moore was allegedly struck by a rifle butt, as were Tom Behan and Jackie Johnston. According to reports from Annie Moore, when the men surrendered Tom Behan was struck with a rifle butt and had his arm broken, so when the captives were ordered into the back of a truck he could not climb aboard as a result. He was struck again on the head with a rifle butt and died at the scene.[8] Behan was a veteran IRA man and at the time of his death was intelligence officer, 1st Eastern Division.

The Free State authorities claimed that Behan was shot while trying to escape through a window in the Glasshouse (so called because of its roof), issuing a statement saying:

> One of the party of men arrested when trying to make his escape from the hut in which he was detained at the Curragh, ignoring the warning of the sentry to desist, was fired on and fatally wounded.[9]

The Glasshouse, where the military prisoners were usually housed, was a small stone and brick military prison on a slight hill, consisting of two floors enclosed within a twelve-foot-high walled enclosure with cells for sixty-four prisoners. During the Civil War and after, it was used as a punishment block for republican prisoners. Mick Sheehan, a republican prisoner from Newbridge, who knew Tom Behan, was in the Glasshouse at the time and thought it highly unusual that an experienced Volunteer like Behan would try to escape through such a small window. It was only some time later that he found out the 'truth'. However, the family of Tom Behan was issued with a death certificate from the coroner of South Kildare stating that he died from shock and haemorrhage due to a gunshot wound to the left side of the head.[10]

Sometime between 13 and 18 December seven of the men were tried before a military court and found guilty of being in possession of arms without authority and sentenced to death. The following official report was issued from the National Army Headquarters, GHQ:

> Stephen White, Abbey Street, Kildare, labourer; Joseph Johnson [sic], Station Road, Kildare, railway worker; Patrick Mangan, Fair Green, Kildare, railway worker; Patrick Nolan, Rathbride, Kildare, railway worker; Brian [sic] Moore, Rathbride, Kildare, labourer; James O'Connor, Bansha, Tipperary, railway worker; Patrick Bagnall, Fair Green, Kildare, labourer, who with others, were arrested at Rathbride, County Kildare, on the 13th inst., were charged before a Military Committee with being in possession, without proper authority, of – 10 rifles, 200 rounds of ammunition therefor, 4 bomb detonators, 1 exploder.
>
> They were found guilty and sentenced to death. The sentence was duly executed this morning, 19th inst., at 8.30 a.m.[11]

It is not known which army unit supplied the firing squad, but it appears that it was brought in from another command, possibly the Dublin Guards – a crack unit formed around members of Michael Collins' old 'Squad'. Commandant Dan McDonnell, senior military police officer, was present at the execution and, at least in the case of Stephen White, was the informant to the registrar of his death.

Before their execution Father Donnelly, chaplain to the troops on the Curragh, administered to the seven condemned men. The seven were shot, one by one. It is said they sang 'The Soldiers' Song' and shook hands with their executioners before being shot. As officer in command, Bryan Moore volunteered to be the last to be executed. This, of course, was harder on him as he had to wait and hear all the shots which dispatched his men. Another priest, Father Mahon, helped to put the remains in coffins. The seven were buried in the yard adjacent to the Glasshouse, but the remains were later exhumed and re-interred in Grey Abbey Cemetery in 1924.

Two of those arrested at Mooresbridge, Pat Moore and Jimmy White, were spared. The question remains why. It is possible that Jimmy White was on guard, slipped his revolver to Annie Moore, and so was not armed. But it was probably a step too far to execute two sets of brothers at the one time. The outcry would have been too great.

Nevertheless, there are many unanswered questions. In a similar situation in County Kerry a group of Volunteers captured under arms was pardoned once they had taken an oath not to attack Free State troops or cause damage to property. Who made the decision regarding the Rathbride column and why? Because of their part in the robberies of local businesses, it is known that the Rathbride column was not well regarded in the locality.[12] (In all stages of the 'troubles' IRA units have resorted to robberies of banks and businesses to fund their campaign and, indeed, for general survival.) Local lore has also claimed that some of the men were involved in the killing of Lieutenant Wogan Browne in February 1922, and that it was an 'unofficial' reprisal for this, but recent research by this author has revealed that none of the Rathbride column was present on that day. It is probable that the executions were the government's way of firmly stamping out insurrection and putting a halt to lawlessness in the area.

Reaction to the mass executions was considerably muted in the local press and no letters of protest were registered, possibly because of censorship. If this had happened under the British regime the county, and country in general, would have been in uproar. Jackie Johnston's mother wrote a scathing letter to the republican newspaper *Éire. The Irish Nation,* in reply to a *Leinster Leader* report, which accused the men of local robberies:

> When he was taken prisoner (no arms been got on his person), he and his companions were cruelly beaten by First Staff Officer (vouched for by an eye witness), tied up with electric wire and taken off to the Curragh to be executed six days afterwards.
>
> His parents received no notification of arrest or execution until long after the foul deed was carried out and the 1st and last letters permitted by him to write were not received until eight days afterwards.
>
> The dugout was described as a huge warehouse containing several tons of food and loot – where in reality it was no more than able to contain the men who were captured, and who used it only as a refuge in any emergency. His mother can emphatically state that her son never did any looting in the surrounding district and was in no way connected with any of the robberies of shops in Kildare as stated in the Press.

These men set out to free their country and not loot – they took an oath to the Republic and kept it, and they gave their young lives to the cause they were devoted to.

Joseph Johnston was eighteen years of age and was praised for his bravery by Father Dominic who served with him on numerous occasions. He was much esteemed by all who knew him and was ever on the alert to do a kindly deed. Comments on the actions of his captors is unnecessary except to say, that, not content with killing their Prisoners of War, did they defame and slander them as well. What can they say to the God when the day of reckoning comes?[13]

There are reports that the men were betrayed and it might not be a coincidence that most of the column was in the one place at the one time. However, other reports say a sentry in the Curragh saw the men crossing the railway on their way to the farmhouse. A large searchlight was mounted on the watchtower of the main military camp and during the hours of darkness the beam from the searchlight lit up the entire Curragh plain. At the time it was quite possible to see the Mooresbridge area from the watchtower, but the Rathbride column would have been aware of this. Another report has it that soldiers had the farmhouse staked out and saw the men going into the stable where the dugout was found.

James O'Connor wrote to his mother:

I am going to Eternal Glory tomorrow morning with six other true-hearted Irishmen.

Patrick Mangan wrote to his mother:

I am to be shot in the morning. I fought for Ireland and am sorry I could not do more … I have made my peace with God and was never so happy as tonight.[14]

On 31 March 1923 the republican newspaper, *Éire. The Irish Nation*, printed the last poignant letters from Bryan Moore, Patrick Bagnall and Paddy Nolan under the title 'Last letters of "executed" soldiers of the IRA':

LETTER OF BRYAN MOORE TO HIS BROTHER.

Hare Park Prison, 18–12–22.

Dear Pat – I am about to die for the Cause of Ireland as many did before. Pray for me and get the children to pray for me. I've just had the priest and will see him again in the morning at 6.30 and receive Holy Communion. He says we are to be envied the deaths we are about to meet, as we shall go straight to Heaven.

Do all you can for Father and Mother. Tell Mary and Kathleen to say a prayer for me every night,

Bryan.

LETTER OF BRYAN MOORE TO HIS MOTHER AND FATHER.

Hare Park Prison, 18–12–22.

Dear Mother and Father – I am about to be executed in the morning and I wish to bid you good-bye, and to ask you to pray for me and the rest of the boys.

I had the priest this evening and will see him again tonight. I am resigned to die. God comfort you both.

Tell Johnny to pray for me. – Your loving Son.

Bryan.

LETTER OF BRYAN MOORE.

Hare Park Prison, 18–12–22.

Dear Johnny – Good-bye, and be good to Father and Mother. Pray for me. – Bryan.

P.S. – You can do a man's part by looking after Father and Mother. Tell them not to worry for me, as I am better off. God bless you.

Dear Annie, – Good-bye. God bless you. Pray for me.

Bryan.

LETTER OF PATRICK BAGNALL TO HIS UNCLE.

Hare Park Prison, 18–12–22.

Dear Jimmy – I hope you and Willie are well. Tell all the boys and girls I was asking for them. I am writing to my sister and father. I am to be shot in the morning, 19th December, at 8.15. Mind Mary and do what you can for her. I know this will nearly kill her. We had a priest who heard our confessions. We are all here, seven of us – Johnston, Mangan, White, Moore, Nolan, Connor [*sic*], and I. We are all to go 'West' together, so don't forget to pray for us. I know you and Willie will be sorry, but it is all for the best, and I hope it sets old Ireland free. We are not afraid to die.

Tell them all in Kildare I was asking for them. Don't forget Harry Moore. We are dying happy anyway. So good-bye old Kildare, good-bye Jimmy and God bless you. I will meet you in Heaven. Tell Tom Byrne I was asking for him. – Your loving nephew, Paddy Bagnall.

The priest's name and address is Father _____, Curragh Camp, a very nice man: you can write him if you want to. He said we will die like men anyway.

Letter of Paddy Nolan to his Father and Mother.

Curragh Camp Prison, 18–12–22.

Dear Father and Mother – I am writing my last few lines to you. I am to be executed to-morrow morning, and I hope you will bear it with the courage of an Irish Father and Mother. I am proud to die for the Cause I loved and honoured, and for which I give up my young life.

Six more of my comrades are to be executed. We have all been to confession and Holy Communion. Father _____ told us we would go straight to Heaven, so do not worry.

Dearest Mother, there are a few pounds in my suitcase, you can have them, or anything else in the house belonging to me.

Loving Father and Mother, good-bye for ever – Your fond and faithful Son.

Paddy.

Father _____, Curragh Camp, sends his sympathies and prayers.

Letter of Paddy Nolan to his Elder Brothers and Sisters.

Curragh Camp Prison, 18–12–22.

My Dear Brothers and Sisters.

Now that I'm about to part from this world, I ask you for one favour – be kind and good to Father and Mother, and never dishonour the Cause for which I die – a Free and Independent Ireland. I bear no ill will to any person. Fond Sisters and Brothers, pray for me. Good-bye forever.

Paddy.

Letter to his Young Brothers and Sisters.

My Dear little ones – I, your fond brother about to pass out of this world, ask you loving little ones to offer up your innocent prayers for me and my comrades on Christmas morning. Be good children, and always obey your parents and do everything in your power to make them happy. God bless you little ones. Good-bye for ever. – Paddy.[15]

Drawing from the Newbridge internee's autograph book, 1923. (Photo: Local Studies, Genealogy and Archives Department, Newbridge Library)

Annie Moore was brought to the women's wing of Mountjoy Jail to join about sixty of her imprisoned comrades. Her brother Bryan and fiancé Paddy Nolan had been two of those executed. Margaret Buckley, who later became president of Sinn Féin from 1937–50, met Annie Moore in Mountjoy just after the executions and described her as 'an inconsolable looking girl'. Another prisoner, Sighle Humphreys, wrote: 'Her story was the saddest of all … if anyone ever got our sympathy she certainly got ours, but I wonder did it give her any comfort.' Annie was transferred to Kilmainham Gaol in February 1923, with the rest of the women republican prisoners, and to the North Dublin Union in April.[16]

The executions caused a lot of bitterness locally on both sides. Both of Mick Sheehan's uncles, who had taken the pro-Treaty side, left the National Army. Captain Patrick Kelly, who had served in the Republican Police, resigned his army commission and went to the Civic Guard. Shortly afterwards, Tom Harris resigned his command and Jim Dunne was appointed to take charge of Kildare Brigade. Dunne reorganised the brigade staff, appointing Jer Dooley, Bracknagh, as adjutant and Seán Cullen, Bracknagh, as quartermaster.[17]

The executions also hardened the hearts of those in the firing line. Kildare Brigade OC Jim Dunne was in action towards the end of the year and recalled:

> In December 1922 I had a report from our intelligence that an enemy intelligence officer visited a dance hall at Johnstown in Kill area. Acting on the information, I went to this hall with one man, a cousin and namesake of my own, who was a member of the Glasgow Brigade and who had come over to fight. While inspecting the hall, we ran into a motor load of CID men and officers from Dublin who had called to the hall to dance. We had no cover and had to stand our ground on the open road. Fire was opened on us at twenty yards by the eight men who comprised the motor load. We returned the fire from our revolvers and, after emptying same, we retreated around a bend in the by-road and on to the main road. As it was 10.30 p.m. and dark at

this time, the enemy did not follow and we escaped unwounded. The enemy lost one officer killed and one CID man wounded. We then rejoined our column and moved about to escape the round up which followed. This ended 1922.[18]

The dead officer was twenty-two-year-old Lieutenant John Keogh, a native of Dublin. An inquest was held the following day at Naas military barracks into the circumstances of his death. According to Commandant Joseph Owens and the other CID men, a shot had penetrated the window of their car as they drove along the Naas Road. The two officers and three CID men went into the dance hall in Johnstown, lined up the thirty or forty men in the hall and searched them. Nothing was found and as they stood beside and near their car a man wearing the uniform of a National Army officer passed by. Commandant Owens followed him and asked him who he was. 'Never mind,' he said, pulling a revolver from under his coat and firing point-blank. Captain Halpin fell as a bullet creased his head. More shots were fired by another man and firing continued for about eight to ten minutes. In the confusion the men escaped. After some time Lieutenant Keogh was found lying dead beside a little river near the Naas Road. His revolver was found to have fired one shot.[19]

10

YOUTHFUL INCENDIARIES

The policy of executions left deep scars on the infant state. Forty republicans were executed between the beginning of December 1922 and the end of January 1923, and in retaliation the IRA began to burn the houses of Free State senators and prominent soldiers of the National Army. During the War of Independence only one house was burned down in County Kildare, but during the Civil War seven houses were burned in the county. However, only two of them are classed as 'big houses' – Palmerstown, the home of Lord Mayo, and Mullaboden, the home of Sir Bryan Mahon – though the others would hardly be described as 'small houses'. Terence Dooley, in *The Decline of the Big House in Ireland*, gives seven houses burned in Kildare during 1922–23.[1] Below is a list of the most expensive houses burned in the county:

    April 1922 – Connaught Lodge. Owner Ernest Northern. Valued at £1,000

    1922 – Russellstown, Athy. Edward Connell. £1,000

    1922 – Blackwood, Robertstown. J. P. Cusack. £1,000

    9 July 1922 – Monasterevin. T. P. Le Fanu and Earl of Drogheda. £3,000

26 November 1922 – Adara House, Ladytown. Mrs Mgt Donnelly. £3,000

30 November 1922 – Lumville, Commissioners of Woods & Forests. £3,000

1922/23 – Rathmuck, Kildangan. T. Cullen. House and furniture. £2,000

1922/23 – Duneany. T. Cullen. House and stables. £2,000

29 January 1923 – Palmerstown House. Lord Mayo. £60,000

23 February 1923 – Mullaboden House. General Mahon. £60,000[2]

During the Truce the IRA in Kildare had commandeered several large country houses, among them Harristown (home of the late Percy La Touché, which had been lying idle for some time), Kildangan and Dowdenstown. There was little damage done to these houses, but their occupation had set a dangerous precedent for the Civil War. When the split occurred in the IRA, big houses were often regarded as safe havens by both sides and where neither side felt they could allow particular big houses to be occupied by the opposing forces, they were burned.[3] From the spring of 1922, houses of British officers, land-owning unionists and substantial-property-owning Catholics had been attacked and burned in County Kildare. On the night of 26 November 1922, Adara House, Ladytown, situated midway between Naas and Newbridge, was destroyed by fire. The house with adjoining land was the property of Mrs Margaret Donnelly, who put in a claim for £3,000. The house was formerly occupied by Colonel Philpotts, but had been untenanted for some years. The caretaker, who lived in the house, left it the previous night having heard men moving about outside and breaking the glass.

The residence of Major Tait at Lumville, Curragh camp, was burned to the ground four nights later. That same night a number of men also set alight the courthouse adjoining Major Tait's residence. The house was a great wooden structure, erected soon after the opening of the Curragh camp in 1855, and owing to the inflammable character of the building, before practically anything could be removed, both courthouse and residence were enveloped in flames. In a short time the whole building and its contents were reduced to ashes. The courthouse was to be used for the new district courts and the adjoining residence, up until the evacuation of the British from the Curragh, was generally occupied by the resident magistrate for the district.[4]

In the various localities, the landed class and loyalists in general, were subjected to increasingly vicious intimidation. Big houses were exposed to incessant raids; demesne walls were pulled down; trees were cut and carted away; livestock was stolen, and the livestock of small landowners was allowed onto the larger estates; and big house employees were intimidated and some even killed. Geographically, there were more big houses burned in every province during the Civil War than in the War of Independence: in Munster, the number rose from forty-two to sixty-nine; in Leinster from eighteen to seventy-four; in Connaught from four to thirty-nine; and in the three Ulster counties from eleven to seventeen. Following Liam Lynch's order to burn the houses of senators, thirty-seven were burned, sixteen of which could be described as big houses.[5]

On 29 January 1923, around thirty armed and masked Volunteers from Naas, Kill and Kilteel, arrived at Palmerstown, Naas, where one of the most important families in the British administration in Ireland in the nineteenth century, the Bourkes (Earls of Mayo and Barons of Naas), lived at Palmerstown House.[6] A leading unionist during the Home Rule campaign, the Earl of Mayo had been nominated by President Cosgrave to the first senate of the

Irish Free State and 'took a great interest in the proceedings of that body'.⁷ According to his obituary:

> The methods of extremists in the disturbances of 1922 and early part of 1923 to intimidate senators and members of the Dáil did not deter him in the pursuit of his duties; but on the contrary, seemed to stimulate him to constant attendance at meetings of the Senate, where he took part in the debates on matters of importance before the Chamber.⁸

The armed men arrived at Palmerstown shortly after the Mayos were finishing dinner. When the men – described as 'youthful incendiaries' – met the Earl of Mayo, an 'orderly officer of the Irish Republican Army' told him that they were going to burn his house in reprisal for the execution of seven anti-Treatyites at the Curragh in December.⁹ However, another of the raiders asked Lady Mayo if her husband was a senator. Members of the same party of raiders may, therefore, have had different motives for burning Palmerstown: some of them may have wished to burn it in response to the government's policy of executions introduced the previous November, while others may have wished to burn it in response to Liam Lynch's order, issued around the same time, that all senators' houses should be burned.¹⁰

The Earl of Mayo asked for time to remove his paintings and the raiders, who 'behaved courteously while in the house', granted him his request, but limited his time to fifteen minutes.¹¹ Only three of the more valuable paintings, the family plate, some of the contents of the housekeeper's room and the study, and clothes belonging to the family were removed. The raiders then saturated the carpets in the main reception rooms on the ground floor with petrol, made the servants pile all the furniture in the middle of each room and sprinkled petrol throughout the house. The windows were then broken, so the fire would take hold. Lord Mayo and a groom named Hurt made futile attempts to extinguish the fire in the dining-room. The military fire brigade from the Curragh camp arrived around midnight, but it was too late. The fire raged throughout the night, floor after floor collapsed with 'deafening noise', and cut-stone window facings and turrets split with the heat, 'flew in splinters' and crashed to the ground. By morning the wine cellar was the only part of the main building that remained undamaged, although the out offices and servants' quarters, built at the northern end of the house, were practically unscathed.[12] As well as the family records, relics from India, Africa, America and Sardinia and a fine collection of furniture were destroyed.[13]

After the fire Lady Mayo was reported as having gone to stay with some friends in the neighbourhood, but Lord Mayo decided to occupy a gamekeeper's cottage on his estate. Asked if he would now go and live in England, he replied firmly: 'No, I will not be driven from my own country.'[14]

In the vast majority of cases the owners of big houses were unable to claim on their insurance as their policies did not cover riot and civil commotion.[15] The Damage to Property (Compensation) Act 1923 allowed landlords, whose houses were burned during the Civil War, to claim for compensation. Lord Mayo's claim was heard at the Naas Circuit Court in early December 1925 before Judge Doyle, KC. Counsel for Lord Mayo, having described in detail the dimensions and architectural style of Palmerstown House as it existed before the burning, said that an agreement had been reached with the state that the amount of compensation for furniture be fixed at £15,000. If they were going to make a proper reconstruction it would be necessary to use Rosenallis sandstone and that would involve extra expense because they would have to go to the quarry where the stone was originally sourced. What they aimed at was the restoration of a house worthy of the occupants, and not more extravagant nor better than the one which was destroyed. The total cost of reconstruction was given as £38,378 6s 2d. Lord Mayo giving evidence said:

> I am the owner of Palmerstown House. I have lived my life there since I became entitled to it. The original building was finished in 1877. The house was lived in by my mother before that in order to superintend the finishing of the interior. I and my family have always used it as a residence and were using it on January 29th as a residence.
>
> Two lads came to the front door and knocked. The door was opened by my butler. One of them made a snatch at his watch chain. The men were disguised. The butler shut the door and came and reported to me that there were two men outside looking for me. The postman arrived from Naas shortly afterwards and came to deliver the letters at the back door. I guessed what was up and I ordered the back door to be locked. That was not done. I then went upstairs for a moment and when I came down the butler informed me that the two men had entered the house and said they were going to burn it. As I had put out the light I asked to have it re-lit so that I could see these two men. One of them appeared to be disguised and I doubt if he were [*sic*] armed. The other man was fully armed with a service rifle. He covered him and me while this individual spoke to me, Lady Mayo then came out of the drawing room and this man who was covered by the armed man said, 'Lord Mayo, I believe is a Senator?' Her ladyship said, 'Yes,' and then she went back to the drawing-room. The man then said, 'We have come to burn the house.' I said, 'Surely you would not burn this house full of beautiful things?' and he said, 'We have our orders, my lord.' I then said, 'Are you going to shoot me?' and he replied 'No, my lord: we are not going to shoot you, but we have our orders to burn the

building.' I said, 'I suppose at all events you will give me twenty minutes for the servants and ourselves to get some wearing apparel while the house is burning?' He said he would. At the end of twenty minutes the place was set on fire. I managed to save pictures that are mentioned in the details of the contents, including three Sir Joshua's, two Titian's and most of my hunting clothes. By that time the incendiaries had entered the dining-room and saturated the thick carpet with petrol and the room was in blazes in a moment. I went and opened the door of the dining-room and I found it a flaming furnace. Nobody has any conception of the fumes from that room – I shall never forget it. I didn't get my throat right for 18 months afterwards. I shut the door and returned to the back hall. There was not a soul there, all had gone outside. Then we were ordered outside ourselves. We went to the garage where we were held up by two raiders. One of the men had an automatic which had the catch down – I asked him to put it up in case a shot would go off – the other had a revolver. The house was then beginning to blaze.

I went into the house again and attempted with a hand-pump to extinguish the fire in the hall but the raiders had done the job excessively well, because not only did they use petrol but also those little pastilles which the Germans used during the war and which are impossible to put out with anything whatsoever. It is only right to say, that the raiders were excessively polite.

By this time I thought it better to call some of my men up. My groom accompanied me to my study, which contained important private papers as well as all the bills of the old house. Every scrap that was in the room was saved by myself and my groom, and also with the help of four very fine looking Free State soldiers who, when they saw the glare in the sky, motored as hard as they could from Newbridge barracks. Things were so bad that I was giving up hopes of saving a piece of furniture that was given to me as a wedding present when my groom said he would fetch it. The soldiers knocked the casement out of the window, which was a rather dangerous operation considering that the rifles were loaded and some of them had the catches down. I have been a soldier six years myself and I told them to put up the catches. The casing was knocked out and eight minutes afterwards my groom left the room having secured the article. A moment later the ceiling fell in and the room was in flames. That is the whole story of what occurred that night.

Replying to Counsel, Lord Mayo said it was a very stormy and wet night. A south-westerly gale was blowing. The old house was very exposed, situated almost like a lighthouse on top of a hill. In summing up Lord Mayo said: 'That is all I have to say in the matter. I know perfectly well who was engaged locally in burning my house.'[16]

The same fate befell the home of Sir Bryan Mahon, at Mullaboden, Ballymore-Eustace. Mullaboden was a splendid two-storey house, erected in the 1850s by Charles Hoffman, who sold it to Colonel Charles Crichton, Lady Mahon's father. Bryan Mahon retired from the British army in 1921 having commanded the 10th Irish Division during the Great War and later served as OC Ireland. He was nominated to the Free State senate in 1922. At 11 a.m. on 23 February, seven men, three wearing National Army uniforms and one in the uniform of a Civic Guard, drove up to Mullaboden House. They were driving a Ford motor lorry, the property of the Anglo-Mexican Petroleum Company, which had been seized several days earlier in Blessington, with seventy tins of petrol, and were armed with rifles and pistols. One man armed with a 'Peter the Painter' pistol was placed on guard at the gate, close to the house of W. J. Mitcheson, the steward, while the rest proceeded to the big house. Mitcheson was asked who lived in the big house and was assured his own house would not be burned. The sentry implied that he was in command of the group. Neither Sir Bryan Mahon nor his wife, Lady Milbanke, were present, having left at the beginning of the month.

The five servants were rounded up by four armed men, who threatened to 'plug' them if they refused to obey orders. The servants, three women and two men, were made to pile the furniture in the centre of each room. The raiders went about the rooms sprinkling petrol and breaking windows with their rifle butts. As the house was catching light the men left, one taking a gramophone on which he put a record. He planted the gramophone on the front steps and set it going. The lively air provided an accompaniment to the crackle of flames in the burning house. Another Volunteer carried out a typewriter, a third field glasses, and a fourth brought out a general's uniform belonging to Sir Bryan Mahon. He coolly donned it and hopped into the lorry with his comrades, who also brought the gramophone. They then drove away warning the servants not to stir from the place.

A fire hose in the yard was turned on the house, but Mr Mitcheson soon saw it was useless to try and save the house and had the hose turned on the servants' quarters and spare rooms, which formed the northern wing of the house, and were almost as imposing a block of buildings as the house with which they were connected. In a half hour the great house was a sheet of flame. National Army troops arrived in an armoured car, as did the Curragh Military Fire Brigade, but it was too late. They saved some of the furniture and silverware, but the estimate of damage was £60,000. Fortunately, the more valuable articles of furniture had been removed to Dublin after the destruction of Palmerstown.

A small party of three National Army troops from Naas under Captain Dowling followed the tracks of the raiders and at Baltiboys they came across about fifteen IRA men, in National Army and Civic Guard uniforms and civilian clothes. The National Army troops opened fire and immediately intense fire was returned. The military sought cover near a cottage and more IRA men arrived to join the fight, calling on the National Army troops to surrender, and trying to surround them. Outnumbered and their ammunition dwindling the National Army troops thought it wise to retire. Under fire Private Smith managed to refill the radiator on his Ford touring car, which had boiled away in the pursuit up the hills. He also managed to turn his car on the road, get it into a place of comparative safety, pick up his comrades and escape back to Mullaboden.[17]

Castletown House, in Celbridge, nearly suffered the same fate. Lady Daisy Fingall recounted its salvation at the last moment:

> ... they came to Castletown. They brought fifty gallons of petrol to burn the house ... the great historical memories were to be laid on the smoking pyre of a new Ireland. Just before the petrol was thrown, a motorcycle came up the long avenue in a great hurry. And a breathless young man, with some mysterious authority, rode into the middle of the group of burners, to say that on no account was the house to be touched that had been built with Irish money by William Conolly, who was Speaker of the Irish House of Commons two hundred years or so earlier.[18]

The man with mysterious authority was thought to be Art O'Connor, but he was imprisoned at the time, so it could possibly have been a brother of his, Seán or Jack, also a prominent member of the local IRA.

Lady Coraile Kinahan, whose father was Captain Charles de Burgh, Royal Navy, of Oldtown, Naas, also recalled an attempt by these 'youthful incendiaries' to burn down the family home:

Mummy stayed a lot at Oldtown during the First War when Daddy was away at Scapa Flow, and she was there during the Irish Civil War when the Sinn Féiners came to burn down the house and were frightened away by grandfather's cold blue eyes and terrifying voice. They made the mistake of sending someone local to do the dirty job and grandfather was a magistrate and recognised them. Mummy said she always slept with a revolver under her pillow then, with which she was a crack shot, having been taught by her brothers.[19]

The owner of Oldtown was General Eric de Burgh, who had retired back to Naas after service in the Anglo-Boer War and the Great War. As well as being a local magistrate, Eric de Burgh took an active part in the County Kildare Archaeological Society, being its president for many years.

On 13 March 1923, a further addition was made to the substantive list of incendiary fires in County Kildare. Hazelhatch post office, situated on the lands of Lord Cloncurry, and within a hundred yards or so of Hazelhatch railway station on the road to Celbridge, was destroyed by fire. Three armed men entered, took some money, sprinkled the office and the residential part of the building with petrol and, ordering the occupants outside, set it alight. The building was a substantial one, erected in 1912 by Lord Cloncurry at a cost of over £600. It served as a receiving and distribution office for letters and parcels in the district. The occupier was Mr Toal, a former head constable of the RIC in Naas, and then a collector of taxes. All official income tax papers and books were lost in the fire, as were all the personal belongings of the family and their pet dog. While the raid on the post office was in progress another party of armed men set fire to the nearby temporary railway signal cabin, erected in place of one destroyed some time earlier.[20]

11

Tintown

The Curragh had been used as an internment camp for republicans since 1916 when Hare Park camp, which had initially been built to billet large numbers of troops during the Great War, was converted for sorting and holding prisoners during the Easter Rising. (The camp took its name because of its location on the edge of the former Kildare Hunt Club site.) For a period the camp was also used to house British recruits to the Royal Irish Constabulary, known as the 'Black and Tans'.[1] While the main internment camp in the War of Independence was located at Ballykinlar, in County Down, further capacity was required to deal with the large number of detainees. To supplement this, the Rath camp on the Curragh was constructed some 400m north-west of the Gibbet Rath to house about 1,500 men. The camp took its name from the historic Gibbet Rath, scene of the massacre of around 350 rebels during the 1798 Rebellion. With the signing of the Treaty and the release of the internees, the huts in the Rath camp were taken down.[2]

Around the second week of July 1922, huts at Hare Park were once again put into use as troops from the National Army arrested local republicans and brought them to the Curragh camp.[3] As the number of detainees grew, further facilities were required and work began on a series of new prisoners' quarters known as Tintown 1, 2 and 3. The site of Tintown was a large complex of huts situated near the cavalry vehicle workshops of today's modern camp, and were actually converted stables clad in corrugated iron (tin), hence the name. Originally constructed to house the large number of horses used in the Great War, the complex had contained a veterinary hospital, horse baths, segregation camp and stables. Tintown No. 1 camp opened in early 1923, with each of the huts originally holding around twenty men. Tintown No. 2 and No. 3 were opened shortly after and were located to the right and left of No. 1 camp. The camps had barbed-wire entanglements and lookout posts for soldiers on guard.[4]

At the start of the fighting, the Provisional Government took a number of steps similar to those employed by the British under the Restoration of Order in Ireland Act (ROIA) and martial law. During the first month of conventional warfare the process surrounding the arrest of republican combatants was straightforward. The taking of prisoners was essentially strategic and by the end of July 1922 at least 2,000 republican prisoners were being held. Initially they were held as 'military captives', but the prisoners demanded to be treated as prisoners of war – the status given by the British during the War of Independence.[5] By August provisions for dealing with the captives during their initial period of detention had been formalised, but the end of the 'open' phase of the conflict, and the changeover to guerrilla tactics, marked the introduction of the Army Emergency Powers Resolution of September 1922, which sanctioned:

> The removal under authority of the Army Council of any person taken prisoner arrested or detained by the National Army to any place or places whether within or without the area of jurisdiction of the

government and the detention or imprisonment of any such persons in any place or places within or without the area aforesaid.[6]

However, the Army Emergency Powers Resolution went further, authorising indefinite detention, though without specifying the relevant criteria. By December 1923 the judge advocate general had approved the details of the new internment forms, but, in the immediate aftermath of the Civil War, the government became concerned that the use of internment might be illegal, particularly as the Free State constitution neither expressly permitted nor forbade it. Subsequently, it was decided to legislate temporarily for this eventuality with the passage of the Public Safety (Emergency Powers) Act in August 1923, which provided for the continued detention of republican internees (see Appendix I).[7]

The Curragh internment camps were plagued with continuous allegations of prisoner ill-treatment, a claim rejected by General Richard Mulcahy. Some weeks after its opening, on 24 April 1923, a number of prisoners escaped through a tunnel from Tintown No. 1 camp, and subsequently a number of tunnels similarly constructed were discovered in Tintown No. 2 and Hare Park camps. It was necessary for the military governor of Tintown No. 2 to ascertain the names of the men who escaped, and in his efforts to do so he met with considerable opposition from the prisoners, the result of orders issued by their leaders. This was allegedly proven by a document found on one of the prisoners containing instructions to hinder any attempt at discipline by the camp regime. To prevent any other escape by tunnel, orders were issued that steps should be taken to make the prisoners dig trenches around each camp at the Curragh. The leaders were removed before the prisoners were made to commence this work, and a number of them were transferred to the military detention prison known as the Glasshouse.[8]

One prisoner, T. Boyle, 'OC republican prisoners Keane Barracks', wrote a letter of protest, which was published in the *Leinster Leader*, about the detention and treatment of two boys, J. Smith (14), Dunlavin, and T. Driver (16), Ballymore, who went on hunger strike in September 1922 for their release.[9] There are no follow-up reports of the outcome, but there were many individual hunger strikes undertaken, and some would have had fatal consequences.

On 1 September 1922, Richard Monks, a republican prisoner from Barrack Street, Kilkenny, was shot dead as he allegedly tried to escape from custody. An inquest was held by Dr J. O'Neill, deputy coroner for South Kildare, and the jury found that the deceased had died from the effects of a bullet wound, fired by a sentry 'in the discharge of his duty'. The Provost Marshal, Commandant Peter O'Mara, deposed that the prisoner had been trying to escape from custody when he was shot dead. A fellow prisoner gave evidence of identification, but no detainees were asked what really happened. This was the first fatality in the Curragh camp.[10]

Internee Alfred McLoughlin wrote to the *Irish Independent* in reply to General Mulcahy's denial of ill-treatment of prisoners in the Glasshouse:

> I am one of the Hare Park prisoners referred to. In spite of what Gen. Mulcahy says, I slept on bare boards in the Curragh military prison for five nights – April 24–28 … I got one blanket … I was handcuffed night and day (day behind, night in front) … The handcuffs were not off for meals; they were off one wrist for alleged dinner, excluding Thursday, April 26, when they were both off for dinner, but on that day I was hanging handcuffed by the wrists to a kit-rack about six inches from the floor for four-and-a-half hours … I was threatened with a gun several times I was to be shot.[11]

Alfred McLoughlin made a sworn affidavit of his treatment in the Curragh. Arrested on 21 October 1922, McLoughlin spent a year interned and was never told why he was being detained.[12]

Peadar O'Donnell arrived from Mountjoy in late December 1922 as a prisoner to the Curragh:

> ... the new camp in the Curragh, Tintown No. 1, which was built to accommodate about 600 men ... Our living huts were large and had concrete floors serrated like stable floors, and we had spring beds. We could cook and distribute our own food and organise the camp life generally.[13]

Discipline, in the beginning was strict, and according to O'Donnell, 'strange as it may sound during my time in Tintown everybody was out, and most of them at [physical] jerks, at 8 o'clock every morning'.[14] The prisoners kept fit with exercises, running, walking and Gaelic football. Rows of huts faced each other throughout the camp, backed by playing fields. Practically the entire Kerry football team was interned there and the camp witnessed some brilliant football matches. The wooden huts contained from twenty to thirty-six men. Very few windows in the huts had any glass and there were gaps in the floor, as all superfluous woodwork was removed for firewood. Winter was very cold, but in summer the camp was pleasant enough.[15]

Tintown was surrounded with heavy rows of barbed wire, with sentry posts on platforms at intervals. At night, prisoners were locked in their huts, powerful lights lit up the limits of the camp and military police patrolled around. During the hours of darkness, the military police unlocked the doors and staged head counts, often flashing lamps on the faces of sleeping prisoners, or pulling down the bedclothes to ensure that a bed was occupied. In the morning, at 7 a.m., the doors were opened and the men went outside for exercises and washed in running water behind a street of huts. Orderlies carried in breakfast, or men prepared their own. Hut inspections were carried out around 10 a.m. and all huts were expected to be clean and tidy, with beds made and all men indoors. The internees stood at ease at the foot of their beds and at the command of their hut leader sprang to attention and numbered off, while National Army officers checked the count. Each hut supplied orderlies for drawing food, for the cookhouse, for fatigue work and for latrine duty. What most prisoners found most difficult was the noise and bustle and the lack of privacy. Escape occupied the minds of most internees and there were many successful bids. Some escaped singly, in disguise, buried under rubbish, or went under barbed wire or over walls.[16]

Much dissatisfaction was voiced about overcrowding, poor food and sanitation, ill-treatment, and indiscriminate use of firearms by prison guards at jails and camps throughout the country. Concern was voiced not only by republican supporters, but also by a number of pro-Treaty senators, among them W. B. Yeats, Lord Granard and Sir Bryan Mahon. Eventually, the complaints prompted the International Committee of the Red Cross (ICRC) to request permission to inspect prisons, internment camps and hospitals and, in April 1923, the request was granted.

On 20 April, the ICRC delegate, R. A. Haccius, visited the Tintown internment camp. In general, his reports were favourable and he concluded that: 'the government refuses the status of "prisoners of war" to prisoners, but in reality treats them as such'.[17] However, there was a fundamental flaw in his reports – he visited Mountjoy Jail, Newbridge and Gormanstown internment camps as well. This experience was similar to Tintown, which elicited the comment that: 'I have not had any complaints to register concerning the food, medical care, or treatment, not having been authorised to question the prisoners.'[18]

A delighted Free State Executive Council published the report, even going to the length of stating that 'prisoners actually receive full prisoner-of-war treatment'.[19] Critics of the government were considerably less enthusiastic about it, and were highly critical of the fact that prisoners were not questioned and that some of the prisons where the most serious complaints had been made were not investigated.[20]

In the immediate aftermath of the Civil War, the Public Safety (Powers of Arrest and Detention) Temporary Act renewed the government's powers of detention for another year.[21] On 1 July 1923, the number of military prisoners in the Free State was officially estimated at 11,316.[22]

12

Peace Comes Dropping Slow

By the end of 1922, the people of Kildare had grown tired of the violence and were intent on getting back to normal. Support for the IRA, never great, continued to wane. The IRA was finding it more difficult to maintain its branches as funds were low, and resorted to robberies of local shops and businesses, further eroding their support. In contrast, support for the Provisional Government continued to increase.

In January 1923, Sinn Féin was reorganised, opening a channel for non-violent activity and giving republicans hope in the advent of a military failure. However, the death toll in the county increased: Private Christopher Sween, Nelson Street, Athy, was killed while on escort duty on 5 January; Private Patrick Lynch died in the Curragh Military Hospital of wounds received in an ambush on 12 January; and Private Joseph Bracken, Naas, lost an eye as a result of wounds sustained in an attack on National Army forces in Wexford.[1] Buoyed by some successes in Munster the IRA prohibited railway workers from assisting the government and much railway property was damaged. In one of the few successful operations in Kildare, Athy barracks was burned down on 23 January, while the Civic Guard barracks at Clane was also burnt.² Another recruitment drive for the National Army brought in hundreds of fresh troops, for the duration of twelve months 'or such shorter period as may be determined by the Army Council'.³ By the beginning of 1923, around 400 National Army troops were stationed in Naas. A column of about forty troops was out on constant patrol, keeping the pressure on the dwindling republicans. The IRA could only operate after dark and republican houses and the homes of friends and sympathisers were raided regularly.

Although the executions provoked a renewed spate of republican violence, it was limited. In March *An tÓglách* reported that the Curragh camp was 'a triumph of efficiency and organisation now equal to any Military Centre in Europe'. *An tÓglách*, with Piaras Béaslaí as editor, had remained loyal to Michael Collins and was now the official organ of the National Army, which maintained it was still the one and only Irish army founded in 1916. Indiscipline and heavy drinking were features of the National Army. Richard Mulcahy sought to redress these problems with a measure of centralisation that had been tried during the War of Independence. The office of Minister for Defence and position of commander-in-chief was an uneasy mixture. He was, however, totally committed to the efficient organisation of the army and to its maintaining high ethical standards and a good reputation.⁴

Apart from its work against republican forces, the National Army was also used for strike-breaking. Heavy-handed tactics were used against farm workers involved in a strike over reduced wages in South Kildare. The secretary of the Athy branch of the Transport Workers Union and most of the men involved in the strike were arrested and interned in Carlow military barracks, along with republican prisoners. The mother of one of the strikers died and he was refused compassionate parole to attend the funeral.⁵

As a further addition to the National Army a Volunteer Reserve had been set up in Newbridge – the first in the country – to give assistance to the military when needed.[6]

On 26 March 1923, Private Pender (20), a native of Derryoughta, Monasterevin, was mortally wounded in an ambush near Valleymount. A military party had left Naas for a routine patrol in Wicklow. Three of them went for a stroll that evening having made their quarters in Valleymount School, when they were attacked by an unknown number of republicans thought to be members of the 'Plunkett Column'. Private Pender died while another soldier was badly wounded.[7]

In April a Civic Guard station was established in Robertstown. County Kildare was well protected by the national police force; the Civic Guard being located in Naas, Newbridge, Kildare, Clane, Kilcock, Rathangan, Robertstown, Athy, Kilcullen, Castledermot and Monasterevin, so that there was no district in the county over which they did not establish a presence.[8] A Civic Guard detachment was later deployed at Kill when one of the new houses for ex-soldiers was taken over as a temporary barracks.[9]

By this time, the republican forces were dwindling rapidly. Only about 8,000 remained in the field, while nearly 12,000 were in prison. Many republicans had begun to accept the futility of further resistance. As a result of the deteriorating situation, the Kildare Brigade was attached to the South Dublin Brigade as a battalion, because it could only muster about fifty active men. The rest had been captured. Their activities had been curtailed to sniping on the Naas Road and at the military barracks.[10]

Most of the IRA leaders realised the hopelessness of their position and urged that the war should be called off, but the chief of staff, General Liam Lynch, maintained that the army was sufficiently strong to continue resistance for an indefinite period.

A meeting of the IRA Executive had been held at Ballymacarbery on 26 March. Several members of the Executive proposed ending the Civil War, but Lynch opposed them and narrowly carried a vote to continue the war. Unable to reconcile their differences, the officers had adjourned for two weeks. On his way back to the planned Executive rendezvous on 10 April, Lynch ran into a force of National Army troops and was mortally wounded.[11]

On 20 April the Executive of the IRA met again and elected Frank Aiken to succeed Lynch as chief of staff, appointing him head of a three-man Army Council. After some discussion, the Executive decided to call on Eamon de Valera, as head of the Republican Government, and Aiken as head of the Army Council, to make peace with the Free State authorities. On 27 April de Valera proposed a negotiated peace, while on 30 April Frank Aiken ordered a suspension of all operations. Negotiations began but failed. On 24 May 1923 Aiken ordered that 'the arms with which we have fought the enemies of our country are to be dumped. The foreign and domestic enemies of the Republic have for the moment prevailed.'[12]

In the meantime seventy republican prisoners tunnelled their way out of the Curragh internment camp on 23 April. The following day National Army troops raided a well-known local republican's house in Celbridge and, after a short engagement, captured six of the escapees, with guns and ammunition. Thirteen-year-old Leo Cardwell was also arrested and brought with the escapees to Naas Military Barracks. The Cardwells were a noted republican family. He was kept apart from the others because of his young age. Later on that night he was admitted to the Curragh Military Hospital suffering from a slight wound to his neck, inflicted by one of his guards. His sister was permitted to see him on 27 April on the condition that she did not ask any questions as to how he came by his wound. A soldier was later court-martialled for the offence. Another sister of Leo Cardwell, Annie (17), had been killed by the accidental discharge of a rifle by a republican visitor in the same house on 7 December 1922.[13]

Other escapees were quickly captured in the Ballymore, Harristown and Naas areas.[14] A number of these who remained free were captured by troops from Naas after an engagement on 15 May in the Wicklow Mountains, in which Neil O'Boyle Plunkett from Burtonport, County Donegal, was killed. O'Boyle Plunkett had escaped from Newbridge in the big breakout of October 1922 and was commander of the Wicklow column. The 'Plunkett Column' – which was made up of men from Dublin, Wicklow and escapees from Newbridge internment camp – had been pursued by troops from Dublin, the Curragh and Naas, and planes from Baldonnel Aerodrome. Five men from the column had been captured the week before after a gun battle, but the remainder had holed up in a small farmhouse at Knocknadruice, in west Wicklow. On 15 May the house was surrounded by about twenty-five National Army troops from Naas barracks, who called on the occupants to surrender. Fire was opened on the farmhouse and returned by the occupants. O'Boyle Plunkett was shot dead in disputed circumstances. The republicans claimed he went out to negotiate a surrender in order to protect three civilians in the house – the owner, her daughter and a local labourer – while the National Army claimed he made a dash from the front door and attempted to jump over a wall when he was shot twice in the head with a revolver.[15]

After the 'dump arms' order of 24 May, the Civil War petered out, though deaths and arrests continued. The peace that followed was an uneasy one. The last execution by the authorities was carried out in June. Many republicans refused to accept the ceasefire and continued to reject the Treaty. Kildare Brigade OC

Jim Dunne and several of his comrades remained on the run until August 1924 when they eventually returned home. Attacks continued throughout the summer and shots were fired at Athy and Castledermot barracks. In Athy the IRA left a mine in the unoccupied Civic Guard barracks, which only partially exploded, causing little damage.[16]

The Civil War had caused great bitterness and division in the country. Around 1,300 people had died: 731 in the National Army, 350 in the IRA and around 200 civilians.[17] (This does not include Northern Ireland where hundreds more civilians, police and military died.) The total financial cost was enormous, around £47 million, a considerable amount of damage being done to buildings, roads, bridges and railways (to the tune of approximately £30 million). War materials, armaments, etc., cost the state around £17 million. Prisoners had to be housed, dependants' allowances had to be paid and, meanwhile, rates and taxes went uncollected in many areas. Communications were destroyed, trade and industry severely damaged, and many businesses collapsed.[18] Claims for damages continued until 1934 when the last claims were settled. By March 1923, Kildare County Council had received claims for damages totalling £214,095. This was exclusive of Lord Mayo's claim for Palmerstown, which was settled for £53,000.[19]

In the jails and internment camps morale plummeted. Around 12,000 republicans still languished behind barbed wire. Many republicans thought the dump arms order was a bluff and that they would again rise in arms to achieve the republic. Republicans could not understand how the Free State had defeated a movement that had, before the Truce, controlled much of the country. The IRA was crushed, as British General 'Bloody' Maxwell observed, 'by means far more drastic than any which the British Government dared to impose during the worst period of the Rebellion'.[20]

On 14 December 1923, republican prisoner Art O'Connor collected signatures from his companions in Kilmainham Gaol. On that occasion he wrote in the album:

What matter who shall reap?
It is our glory and our pride
To tend the growing corn
To wait the coming morn
Be dead, perhaps, before the Harvest tide
While others shameless sleep.[21]

As the political situation began to stabilise throughout 1923, it was formally decided to begin the release of internees in small groups, once they had given written undertakings not to resume subversive activities, but it was a slow process. Tensions inside the jails and camps simmered and eventually brewed over with drastic results.

13

Hunger Strike, Murder and Mutiny

Despite the ending of hostilities, thousands of republicans languished in jails and internment camps awaiting release. In April 1923 the Free State authorities had removed a ban on parcels and letters, and prisoners were allowed one letter per week. As a result of continued dissatisfaction over demobilisation in the National Army, the government deemed it inappropriate to release all the republicans still held in camps and prisons throughout the country. By mid-October, tension was building among the imprisoned republicans because of the conditions in the jails and camps in which they were incarcerated, and because they were still imprisoned with no release in sight. On 13 October the prisoners in Mountjoy Jail resolved to begin a hunger strike to highlight their demands and alleviate their plight. In Mountjoy Jail, 420 men, ten of whom were members of the Dáil, went on hunger strike. An order of the day was issued by Frank Aiken, IRA chief of staff, asking for support for the Mountjoy hunger strikers, which was interpreted in the jails and internment camps as an invitation to support the Mountjoy prisoners by joining the strike, and thousands of prisoners decided to do so.

The prisoners in Kilmainham and in other jails and camps followed their example immediately, and the strike soon spread to other centres. Within a matter of days 7,033 republicans were on hunger strike. The figures given by Sinn Féin at the time were: Mountjoy Jail 462; Cork Jail 70; Kilkenny Jail 350; Dundalk Jail 200; Gormanstown camp 711; Newbridge camp 1,700; Tintown 1, 2, and 3, Curragh camp 3,390; Hare Park camp 100; and, 50 women in the North Dublin Union. On 18 October over 100 men were removed from Mountjoy to the Curragh in an effort to break the strike, but it had the opposite effect as the prisoners there joined in. However, a mass hunger strike was difficult to manage and many could not stay on it. By this time, however, earlier hunger strikes had taken the lives of several internees.

An earlier hunger strike by women prisoners in February 1923 had led to their release, but the Free State authorities were so disgusted at having been forced to concede to the hunger strikers' demands that a motion was passed in parliament outlawing the release of prisoners on hunger strike. There had been a short hunger strike in the Curragh in June 1923 and Daniel Downey, Dundalk, died in the camp's hospital wing on the tenth of that month. Although the hunger strike had ended before he died, the short fast, combined with the general ill-treatment meted out to prisoners, proved fatal.

General neglect was largely to blame for the deaths of several hunger strikers: Frank O'Keefe from Tipperary, who died in the Curragh camp sometime in 1923; Matthew Ginnity from Birkenhead, England, who died on 23 July in Tintown No. 2; and Dick Hume, Wexford, who, although not on hunger strike, died on 9 November, after being brought from Tintown No. 3 to the Curragh Military Hospital.[1] On 2 September Joseph Whitty (19) of Wexford died on hunger strike in the Curragh camp. Despite the earlier deaths, 1,300 internees in the Curragh joined the Mountjoy hunger strikers.²

Ernest Blythe, Minister for Finance, visited the hunger strikers in Newbridge and, on meeting some of them, advised them to end their protest:

> We are not going to force feed you, but if you die we won't waste coffins on you. You will be put in orange boxes and you will be buried in unconsecrated ground. So have sense and come off it.³

A number of prisoners saw the hunger strike as futile once it became evident that a process of phased releases was about to commence. Nevertheless, some inmates continued their hunger strike to the bitter end. Two more prisoners died: Andy O'Sullivan and Denis Barry.

On 11 November, Commandant Denis Barry, Blackrock, Cork, died in the Curragh Military Hospital after thirty-four days' hunger strike, having been brought there from Newbridge camp. Richard Mulcahy stated that Denis Barry's remains would be interred within official premises of the state and he was buried in the confines of the internment camp. Within five days the decision was reversed as Barry had not been convicted of a crime. His remains were handed over to relatives and the body lay in state overnight in Newbridge Town Hall. The remains were removed the following day to Cork, where the body was refused entry to a local church. The remains lay overnight in the rooms of the Cork City Executive of Sinn Féin at Grand Parade. The funeral to the Republican Plot at St Finbarr's Cemetery in Cork the next day was attended by a large number of people. At the cemetery republican David Kent – no clergyman being permitted to attend the funeral – sprinkled the grave with holy water and recited the last prayers before the coffin was lowered into the earth.⁴

While they ignored other hunger strikes, the government understood that because of the number of republicans on the protest this hunger strike was different. If too many deaths occurred, public opinion would swing away from the state to the republican movement and could jeopardise what little stability there was. The large number of prisoners on hunger strike was a problem not only for the Free State authorities, but also for the IRA leadership. The Executive had little say in the strike, being informed about it only after it had begun. Some IRA officers within the prisons, such as Liam Pilkington and Joe Harrington, sought to limit the number joining the protest, but their request was turned down in case it caused bitterness among the prisoners if one was picked over another. The IRA Executive, in consultation with the OCs of the prisoners in each prison, left the decision to join the protest or not to each prisoner, but issued orders that those physically unfit should not take part. Within weeks many were drifting off the protest, but by the end of October there were still 5,000 on hunger strike, determined to achieve their aims.[5]

Owen Boyle, Donegal, died in custody in Newbridge camp on 13 November. One week later it was stated that the official numbers of prisoners held was down to 6,800, of whom 230 were still on hunger strike. The authorities still refused to grant concessions to the POWs even after the deaths, and the IRA command in the jails ended the hunger strike on 23 November. After forty-one days the strike had collapsed without any definite promise of release.

Republican leaders Tom Derrig and David Robinson, held in Kilmainham, and Liam Hearty, held in Mountjoy, visited the hunger strikers in Hare Park, the Curragh and Gormanstown, directing them to finish their protest. Though the strike itself failed, it did set in motion a release programme for the prisoners – over 5,000 had already been released – the state was afraid of a repeat of the strike the following year. Soon afterwards all women prisoners and a number of the men were released. Conditions for those remaining improved to an extent. However, some of the prisoners had fasted for fifty-five days and many men and women were in a precarious state of health, from which they never recovered. They suffered afterwards through overeating and taking food without medical supervision, while still in custody. One particular prisoner, Joseph Lacey, Wexford, continued to decline after the end of the hunger strike, and died a month later on Christmas Eve in the Curragh camp.[6] On 12 December, *Éire. The Irish Nation* reported:

> Reports from Tintown No. 3 to the effect that the men on list appended are in a condition of health that would make further detention very dangerous. They are quite unfit to endure the remaining winter months; the cold and hardship of camp life in their reduced state will seriously aggravate their respective complaints.
>
> The treatment on the whole of the men who came off the strike in this camp has been fairly good, but we must take exception to the diet and to those who came off strike at periods varying from 14 to 35 days. Those who came off on the 14th or 15th day (about 850) got, for their first meal one pint of Bovril; their next consisted of tea and stale bread, which had lain in the stores during the first fortnight of the strike. After that, ordinary diet.
>
> On the 23rd day of the strike 40 men came off. These were sustained for two or three days on suitable diet and then put back on ordinary prison fare. As a result of such ill-treatment, combined with insufficient heat, draught and overcrowding, a large number of these men are suffering from dyspepsia, rheumatism, bronchial trouble, and even tuberculosis of the lungs. One man, Joe Gibbons, Woodstock Street, Athy, who went off strike on the 23rd day, was removed to the military hospital suffering from acute tuberculosis. There is no

further information to his condition. There were several prisoners in this camp in whom there was a tendency to tuberculosis and kidney disease. These troubles have become acute in some of them since the strike. The supply of medicines has been all along irregular.[7]

When the hunger strike finally collapsed, the discipline, which had held the prisoners together, began to erode also. Todd Andrews wrote that the will to escape had gone and that interest in the Irish language had disappeared and nobody spoke or tried to learn Gaelic.[8] In the jails and camps it was widely admitted that the strike's collapse had a demoralising effect. The end of the strike was a let-off for the government. A large number of deaths could have produced a considerable sympathetic reaction in the tradition of republican martyrdom and in the immediate aftermath there was an increase in the number of prisoners released. However, the government decided that a mass release policy would have made it appear that the protest had been a success. In the ensuing months the question of a general amnesty was often debated but always rejected in favour of the 'dribble' policy, in which prisoners were let out slowly. In some instances, officers were released and the men retained. This was designed to disillusion the internees. The programme of gradual release was completed in the summer of 1924 and after that time only those convicted for criminal acts remained. Ernie O'Malley, who was transferred to Tintown in April 1924, recalled that the men were released until only the senior officers were left and these were freed in batches of two: 'The enemy could not be gracious, even after two years of imprisonment, and we cursed them heartily as we waited. They wanted to avoid an organised welcome to the prisoners; that could mean they were losing ground.'[9]

A small group of prominent republicans were held in the

Glasshouse, among them Mick Sheehan, who had taken part in the mass hunger strike. He was one of the last to be released, as were leaders such as Art O'Connor, Ernie O'Malley, Gerry Boland and Tom Derrig. These were released in ones and twos to counter any public celebration of their release.[10] The sentenced prisoners known as 'Mullaney's column' were all released in June 1924: Pat Mullaney and Michael O'Neill, Leixlip; Jack O'Connor, Celbridge; Tom Cardwell, Celbridge; Jim Dempsey, Celbridge; and Tim Tyrell, Maynooth. They were released unconditionally and returned to their homes on the train. The return of the prisoners was unexpected and was taken locally to indicate that there were major differences in government circles with regard to the releases. They were paraded in Tintown and informed that the governor general had exercised his powers of clemency to remit the whole sentences. Mullaney had been sentenced to ten years, while the rest were all serving seven-year sentences.[11] The last sentenced prisoners were not released until December 1926, and they included five National Army soldiers held in the Glasshouse, who had helped republicans.[12]

Despite the dwindling prison population – December 1923 saw the highest release of prisoners countrywide – trouble continued in the Curragh internment camp and, in December, a military policeman suspected of carrying information to republican prisoners was murdered. The body of Corporal Joseph Bergin (23), from Camross, County Laois, was found in the canal at Milltown Bridge on 15 December. The medical evidence showed that he had suffered considerable violence, and been shot six times in the head.

Bergin was an IRA intelligence officer and had been attached to GHQ during the War of Independence. He was identified carrying messages in and out of Tintown No. 3 on behalf of prisoners there. Colonel M. J. Costello, director of military intelligence, ordered

Captain James Murray to investigate the allegations against Bergin, a military policeman. Bergin was intercepted returning to the camp by several National Army officers, brutally interrogated and tortured in a hut and, while still alive, tied to the rear of a car and dragged behind at speed. His body was then dumped in the Grand Canal. Bergin's girlfriend, Peg Daly, knew he was dead when his blood-stained cap was thrown into her hallway in Kildare town. The newspapers commented:

> Bergin's murder was only one of nearly a hundred. He was slain as a beast would be slain. Many others were done to death in the same terrible way. In many cases, as apparently in Bergin's, the victims were first tortured, and then killed, usually because they would not betray their fellows.[13]

Not long after the killing, Captain Murray fled to Argentina, leaving his wife and children behind. A year later he returned to Dublin, having been persuaded to come back for a normal jury trial. Murray was arrested and discharged from the army. Described as an ex-intelligence officer in the National Army, he was charged with Joseph Bergin's murder in the Dublin District Court in January 1925. His trial began on 9 June at the Central Criminal Court. Murray claimed he was a scapegoat. (It was believed Murray was the leader of a group of National Army troops responsible for several murders during and after the Civil War, including that of Noel Lemass.)

James Cleary, a soldier, in evidence for the prosecution, stated that on 13 December 1923, Colonel Michael J. Costello had ordered him to give a car to Captain Murray. When the car was returned to him the following day, 'it was covered in blood on the inside'. On 17 December, Private Cleary was detained and held in

Arbour Hill for four months 'in safe custody'. Cleary was never told on what charge he was held, only that it was not safe for him to be at large.[14]

Colonel Costello was called to give evidence and he stated that Corporal Bergin was 'in illicit communications with the Irregulars and with republican prisoners in Tintown'. He claimed he had sent Captain Murray, who was on his staff, to investigate. In the course of the trial it emerged that Costello had assisted Murray in leaving the country. The case of Noel Lemass, murdered in the Dublin Mountains in July 1923, was mentioned when Captain Murray blurted out an admission that his brother had had a similar experience. His brother, Michael Murray, an army commandant, had been asked to take the blame for the killing of Noel Lemass, he said, but had refused. Now, he was being asked to do the same.[15]

He did not, however, convince the jury. James Murray was found guilty of the murder of Joseph Bergin and sentenced to death on 12 June. An appeal was lodged, and on 1 July it was heard in the Court of Criminal Appeal. Produced in the appeal were four letters, which Murray claimed he had written to Colonel Costello when he was in Argentina, and a confession attributed to Murray, concerning the death of Bergin. In the letters Murray phrased his words to suggest he had been acting on orders, but he did not want to incriminate anyone else. He requested a settlement of the affair as he 'did not want to be a hunted man' for the rest of his life. If he did not get a suitable response to his requests he said he would surrender himself for trial. The confession, which was only produced at the end of the trial, outlined the instruction, which Murray claimed had been given to him by Costello in the presence of Murray's brother, Michael. It mentioned that the colonel said that Bergin was dangerous and had to be shot. A car to take Murray and two unidentified men to the Curragh was arranged by the colonel, and Bergin was apprehended in Kildare and taken to an unoccupied house at Thomastown to be questioned and searched. Incriminating documents were found on him, and he admitted to being involved with the IRA. Then 'Bergin was shot and his body taken to Milltown Bridge and thrown in the canal'.[16] Murray reported back to Costello, and it was agreed that he should go away for a while, and that the colonel would arrange the care of Mrs Murray and her children. Mrs Murray received the weekly pay of her husband while he was abroad.

The court had to weigh the evidence of Captain Murray against the denials of Colonel Costello. Murray claimed that, in fact, he had not gone to Kildare at all on the evening of the murder, as he was suspicious of the purpose of the excursion. The state held that the letters from Argentina were designed to implicate Costello, and thus cause the government not to arraign Murray for murder. The prisoner denied having written the 'confession', though he admitted that the writing was like his. An army handwriting expert swore all five documents were by the same hand. The appeal failed and Murray was returned to Maryborough (now Portlaoise) prison. Four days before he was due to be hanged his sentence was commuted to penal servitude for life.[17] James Murray died in Maryborough prison in July 1929. His health was fair on committal, but he had a history of tuberculosis and had been in a sanatorium. The cause of death was pulmonary tuberculosis.[18] His wife and daughters went to live in England. Costello retired from the army in 1945 with the rank of major general and became a successful businessman. He died in 1986.[19]

The Bergin case continued to be an embarrassment for the National Army when, in October 1925, Joseph Mack, described as a former lieutenant, was charged with Bergin's murder. Mack was well known in Kerry where he was involved in Civil War excesses in the Killarney region. Several days later Sergeant John Dooley was charged with involvement in the Bergin murder, but a week later the charges were dropped against him.[20] Joseph Mack was found not guilty of murder in April 1926.

After the dump arms order some republicans could not face the fact that the war was over and remained on the run. Others settled back into a life without fear of arrest or death. For some it was years since they had worked and now they settled down to rearing a family and earning an income. Gus Fitzpatrick, Naas, and Bill Gannon, Kildare, former internees, went on to play for the Kildare football team and were on the winning side when Kildare won the 1927 and 1928 All-Ireland Championships. (On the morning of the game news came through of the death of that great Irish patriot, Kildare man John Devoy, at the age of eighty-six in Atlanta.)[21] The GAA played a vital role in the reconciliation after the Civil War. The GAA playing fields were neutral grounds where former enemies could meet. In the great All-Irelands of 1927 and 1928, Jack Higgins, a National Army man who had served in the Curragh, played alongside IRA men Gus Fitzpatrick and Bill 'Squires' Gannon with Kildare against the Kerry team, which fielded Con Brosnan, a captain in the National Army, and John Joe Sheehy, a former IRA Volunteer and one of the greatest footballers of his time. Although most matches passed off peacefully, some isolated incidents stand out. Peter Pringle, Rathangan, recalled how revolvers were produced at a tournament game in Clonbullogue because of some rough tackling by a Rathangan man on a local player.[22]

Jim Collins of Kilcullen had remained staunchly anti-partitionist throughout the Civil War, undergoing imprisonment in seven prisons including Kilmainham, Dundalk, the Curragh and Mountjoy. One of his favourite stories was of his escape from Dundalk prison in the company of Frank Aiken at the beginning of the Civil War. Jim was recaptured in Meath and, having served his final term of imprisonment (in Newbridge), was released on Christmas Eve 1924. Walking from Newbridge to Kilcullen that night and seeing no lights in the town on his arrival was an experience often described by Jim as one of the darkest and loneliest of his life. He had not been home for a number of years and he discovered, after his time 'on the run', that many of his friends had left the area, some to go to America. Jim's family had kept the corn mill at Kilcullen since 1880 and his father had earned most of his living providing feed for British army horses on the Curragh. It was ironic that Jim, an only child, should grow to be so proud of being a member of the 6th Battalion of the Carlow Brigade, IRA.[23]

On the opposite side, the National Army emerged from the Civil War in very poor condition, its ranks swollen with virtually untrained recruits, its public standing blighted by reports of murders and atrocities, and its future in doubt. In the aftermath of the Civil War, its strength was reduced from 60,000 to half that figure, both to cut costs and to bring the force to a manageable peacetime size. Not everyone was satisfied with the demobilisation and the fact that some ex-British army officers and 'trucers' were retained in service caused further annoyance. (In April 1922, Emmet Dalton, an ex-British soldier, had invited veterans of the Great War to raise and train a new army for the Free State.) Many of the former IRA men within the army were not happy with the demobilisation and officers who had completed the officers' training programme in the Curragh were among the first group to be demobbed.

On 9 November 1923, seven officers refused to accept their demobilisation papers. They were arrested and court-martialled, causing the unrest to spread to other officers at the camp. Joe Maher, Cullinagh, who had led the IRA ambush at Barrowhouse in 1921, had enlisted in the National Army and become a military policeman. He was one of the many who resigned when a number of ex-British servicemen were given appointments as NCOs. Lieutenant Jim Sheehan, Newbridge, was also demobbed.[24]

Disaffection continued until the following March when Major General Liam Tobin and Colonel Charles Dalton presented an ultimatum to the government. They alleged that the government was not attempting to bring the Free State any closer to being a republic, and demanded the reorganisation of the army, suspension of demobilisation and the removal of the Army Council. The ultimatum also reproached the government for abandoning the quest for unity. Liam Cosgrave read the ultimatum to the Dáil on 11 March 1924. He considered this to be an 'army mutiny' and acted swiftly to crush the opposition to the elected government. On the same day Joseph McGrath resigned as Minister for Agriculture and Commerce. The signatories to the ultimatum withdrew their threat the following day, and explained that their object had been achieved, while President Cosgrave announced that an inquiry would be held.

On 18 March the Army Council – consisting of Adjutant-General Gearóid O'Sullivan, Seán MacMahon, the chief of staff, and Seán Hurley, the quartermaster general – brought the mutiny to a head by ordering the arrest of the leading mutineers, who were meeting in a Dublin hotel. The revolt, for the most part, was confined to officers, and those involved were arrested and others forced to resign. Before the mutiny had ended, fifty-five officers had absconded with their weapons and ammunition, and forty-nine others, including three major generals and five colonels, had resigned. The casualties included Richard Mulcahy, who resigned as Minister for Defence, and three senior officers of the Army Council. The crisis simmered until October but a combination of strong measures by Kevin O'Higgins, vice-president of the Executive Council, sensible words behind the scenes, and generous gratuities in some cases, concluded the mutiny. All the men let go were guaranteed pensions in recognition of their services and many found jobs in the Civil Service or the Garda Síochána.[25]

In the autumn of 1924, the National Army was finally established on a permanent legal and constitutional footing through the Defence Forces Act. Ambiguities about allegiance were disposed of by a ban on membership of oath-bound bodies. Of the four barracks in the county only the Curragh and Kildare town were occupied by the army. (The Civic Guard had moved to Dublin Castle.) By 1928, the decorative emblems of the British were removed from the Curragh camp and the barracks were renamed after the signatories of the 1916 Proclamation: Pearse, MacDonagh, MacDermott, Plunkett, Clarke, Connolly and Ceannt. By 1932, owing to the lack of interest of successive governments, the army's strength had fallen to fewer than 6,000 men and for the next few years remained that size.

For republicans 'the Cause' was not lost and enough Volunteers remained to invigorate a new IRA. On 19 June 1925, 8,000 marched to Bodenstown to hear an oration by Eamon de Valera. The following year, on 16 April, the County Kildare Easter Commemoration was held at the Grey Abbey churchyard, where Seán Lemass, TD, delivered an impressive oration at the republican plot where the seven men executed in the Curragh during the Civil War were buried (they were re-interred there in 1924). Relatives of the executed men were present. Speaking at the conclusion of the oration by Lemass, one of the mothers said that the 'mothers and relatives of these men would be prepared to give them up again in the same cause and they were proud that their sons had given their lives bravely for the Republic'.[26] A large force of Civic Guards and detectives watched the proceedings and stayed in the churchyard until everyone had left. Less than a month later Patrick Murphy, Naas Road, Newbridge, was charged at Naas with having on his premises a revolver 'with intent to endanger life or cause serious injury to property'; the IRA had not gone away.[27]

Conclusion

Estimates of the strength of the IRA during the Civil War range from 20,000–25,000. A report compiled for the IRA leadership in August 1924 gave an estimate of 14,541 members, but these figures are misleading, the IRA's calculations being based on strength on paper, rather than on active membership.[1] Initially, the pro-Treaty forces stood at between 7,000 and 14,000, but as the National Army was developed as a regular army from its inception, its ranks swelled to 60,000 by the end of the Civil War. (There was another important difference – the anti-Treaty forces could only muster 3,000 rifles, whereas even before the start of the fighting the pro-Treaty forces had received nearly 12,000 rifles, together with ammunition, machine guns and armoured cars from Britain.[2]) On 4 July 1922, the Provisional Government issued a call to arms. The response was overwhelming and, on the first day of recruitment, as huge queues formed outside the centres, recruitment officers were unable to deal with the number of applicants. There were many reasons for this. Unemployment had reached 150,000 and there were thousands of demobbed British soldiers anxious and willing to continue a way of life to which they had grown accustomed. There were also many youths coming of age who had a desire to emulate the exploits of an earlier generation.[3] The vast proportion of National Army recruits were not, and had not been, members of Sinn Féin or of the old IRA.[4] Calton Younger, in *Ireland's Civil War*, wrote:

> There were bad hats among the rival armies; both sides employed 'trucers' or 'trucileers', men who had taken no part in the War of Independence but had swarmed into the IRA during the long Truce for reasons often, though not always, reprehensible. Some were youngsters only now of age to join and full of idealism, others were opportunists and some were criminals. In any event, their entry into the IRA had been unfortunate for it is doubtful if the old IRA, however divided, could have fought each other to the death if the influx of strangers had not thinned their comradeship.[5]

Mooresbridge, Kildare, was raided many times by crown forces during the War of Independence and also by the National Army during the Civil War. Annie Moore, whose brother Bryan and fiancé Paddy Nolan, were executed at the Curragh, said the behaviour of the Free State troops was much more brutal than that of the British.[6] Much of the bitterness and hatred that led to outrages can be traced to personal animosity and the settling of old scores. Dozens of ex-British soldiers had been shot dead during the War of Independence. Now many former British soldiers were wearing the new uniform of the National Army. With the death of Michael Collins the bitterness increased. The spirit of compromise vanished from the leaders of the Provisional Government and was replaced by a ruthless intransigence; the main reason why the IRA was defeated.

Another reason behind the republican's defeat was the repressive policy of the Free State Government regarding prisoners. The British Government and intelligence system had been fighting a war blindfolded. The main difficulty experienced throughout was found to be one of identity. The British did not know who they were looking for, or even arresting, whereas the Provisional Government knew exactly who to look for. They knew all the activists, their friends and relations, their safe houses and hangouts, and could make more coordinated and decisive arrests than the crown forces. The main intent of internment was to remove an organised and potential threat. Its success can be measured in the recognition that the repressive Free State policy was partly responsible for the defeat of the IRA, which was accomplished in a short space of time; something Britain could not achieve over a longer time frame.

Throughout the Civil War, and for some time after, thousands of republican prisoners lingered inside the camps and jails, their release pending on the whim of the Provisional Government. Inside the camps the harsh prison regime was responsible for brutality, medical neglect, the stoppage of vital food parcels, the shootings of would-be escapees, executions of those arrested under arms and the brutal murder of at least one republican. When hostilities had long ceased and their release was not forthcoming, the prisoners embarked on a hunger strike. This protest failed in its objective owing to government intransigence and led to the death of several internees. The failure of the strike and the continuing incarceration of prisoners led to a further demoralisation among republicans, most of whom, as internees, had no release date in sight. The discipline that had held them together began to erode. Prisoner releases were indiscriminate. In further moves to break morale and organisation individual officers would be released, then the rank and file, then officers again. The sense of cohesion began to be lost and, as Ernie O'Malley said, 'The majority of us were aimless and loafing.'[7] On the outside, prisoners' families and their dependants were impoverished and the government's repressive conditions continued as long as resistance lasted. All these conditions contributed to the demoralisation of the IRA and contributed to its defeat.

In County Kildare republicans were in the minority, fighting against overwhelming odds. Crown forces had been replaced by the

National Army and the Civic Guard, many of whom were recruited locally. Unlike the few crown force casualties in the 1916–21 period, the majority of the National Army troops killed in the county in 1922–23 were from local families, further alienating the population from the republicans.

The material damage inflicted in the county by republicans was more widespread and discriminate than the previous campaign, and while it was a testament to the increasing tactical capabilities of the IRA, it did not endear them to the local populace, from where they should have drawn support. The majority of people just wanted a return to normality and peace at any price.

APPENDIX I

SAORSTAT ÉIREANN.

Public Safety (Emergency Powers) Act, 1923.
Public Safety (Emergency Powers) No. 2 Act, 1923.

302

ORDER BY THE MINISTER FOR DEFENCE.

WHEREAS *Michael Sheehan Newbridge Kildare* (hereinafter referred to as the prisoner) was at the date of the passing of the PUBLIC SAFETY (EMERGENCY POWERS) ACT, 1923, detained in Military Custody,

AND WHEREAS the prisoner was not before the passing of the said Act sentenced to any term of imprisonment or penal servitude by any tribunal established by the Military Authorities,

AND WHEREAS I am of opinion that the public safety would be endangered by the prisoner being set at liberty,

NOW I RISTEARD UA MAOLCHATHA an Executive Minister within the meaning of the said Act do hereby order and direct that the prisoner be detained in custody under the said Act until further order but not after the expiration of the said Act.

Dated this 9th day of August, 1923.

Signed RISTÉARD UA MAOLCATA,
Minister for Defence.
Member of the Executive Council of Saorstat Eireann.

Copy of internment order for Michael Sheehan, Newbridge 1923.
(Author's collection)

Appendix I

List of Kildare prisoners in Newbridge internment camp at 8 p.m. on 5 December 1923 (source: Military Archives, Dublin):

James Bean, Moortown, Celbridge

John Burke, Roseboro, Naas

Thomas Cardwell, Celbridge

William Clifford, Newtown Villa, Kilcullen

James Colton, Abbey Street, Kildare

John Cotter, Celbridge

Edward Donovan, Ballybush, Straffan

Thomas Doran, Kilcullen

Richard Fitzgerald, Feerane, Suncroft

Augustine Fitzpatrick, Railway View, Naas

Peter Gill, The Knocks, Naas

Walter Halligan, Railway Bridge, Naas

John Hayden, 41 Duke Street, Athy

Patrick Kavanagh, Castledermot

Patrick Kelly, Narraghmore

Peter Kelly, Corduff

James Kenny, Dunbrin, Athy

Joseph Knight, Old Grange, Monasterevin

Maurice Lambe, Kilcullen

Peter Lambe, William Street, Athy

Thomas Lynam, Clongorey, Newbridge

James Mackey, Sallymount, Brannockstown

Joseph Martin, Old Grange, Monasterevin

Patrick Martin, Old Grange, Monasterevin

James McNamara, Athy

Bernard Melia, Ballygraney

Henry Myers, Kilcullen

Patrick Nelligan, Monasterevin

Patrick O'Carroll, Sallins Road, Naas

James O'Connor, Inchaquire, Ballitore
Michael O'Kelly, Gleann na Greine, Naas
James O'Rourke, Athy
Michael O'Rourke, Canal Harbour, Athy
Lawrence O'Toole, Spratstown, Collinstown
William Pender, Ticknevin
Pat Quinn, Halverstown
Seán Rafferty, Naas
Michael Ryan, Brackna, Rathangan
Michael Sheehan, Newbridge
Martin Tracy, Walterstown
Nicholas Twomey, Ballymore-Eustace
James Wynne, Ballymen, Athy

List of Kildare prisoners transferred from Gormanstown to Newbridge on 30 November 1923 (source: Military Archives, Dublin):

James Brady, Church Street, Kilcock
James Collins, Main Street, Kilcullen
Peter Crinnigan, Coolayne, Carbury
Richard Dunne, Greenhills, Kill
James Kelly, Kilteel, Rathmore
John King, Finnerty, Maynooth
Thomas Mangan, 3 Leinster Cottages, Maynooth
Thomas McKenna, Barberstown, Straffan
James Melia, Ballygarnet, Ballygraney
Thomas Melia, Ballygarnet, Ballygraney
Christopher Mills, Killinmore, Kill
Peter Mills, Painstown, Kill
Patrick O'Brien, Prumplestown, Castledermot

Appendix I

Patrick Siney, Kill, Monasterevin

Patrick Woods, Furryhill, Kilteel

List of Kildare prisoners released from Newbridge camp, July–December 1923, with some dates of when they were released (source: Military Archives, Dublin):

James Behan, Lughill, Monasterevin

James Brady, Celbridge, 19 November

Patrick Brennan, Lughill, Monasterevin

John Burke, Roseboro, Naas, 13 December

William Butterfield, Main Street, Naas, 15 August

Denis Byrne, Tussagh, Monasterevin, 19 November

Vol. Caulfield, Newbridge Barracks

John Conlon, Clongorey, Newbridge, 9 October

Andrew Conroy, Ballyneagy, Monasterevin, 24 November

Richard Conway, Narraghmore, Ballitore, 5 November

Charles Curran, Kilcullen

Hugh Curran, Halvertstown, Kilcullen

James Donnelly, Dispensary, Monasterevin, 23 July

Frank Driver, Ballymore

Matthew Duffy, Mountrice, Monasterevin

Thomas Gaffney, Abbey Street, Naas, 18 August

Joseph Gavin, Market Street, Newbridge, 10 September

J. Harris, Caragh, 8 October

William Harris, Prosperous

Patrick Hollywood, Kealestown, Leixlip

James Kavanagh, Ballitore, 30 November

P. Kehoe, Narraghmore, Ballitore

Peter Kelly, Ballinafagh, Prosperous

Thomas Kelly, Rathangan

Alfred Mangan, Celbridge, 8 September
Thomas McCabe, Balrinnet, Carbury, 5 September
James McCaul, Newbridge
Thomas Murphy, Cookstown, Ballitore, 19 November
Fred Noone, Dublin Road, Naas, 13 August
Peter O'Brien, Garterfar, Castledermot. Released 30 August, on medical grounds – pulmonary tuberculosis and general debility – refused to sign release form
James O'Connor (Colton), Abbey Street, Kildare, 4 September
Michael Perkins, Naas, 3 September
William Perkins, The Square, Monasterevin, 20 September
Edward Tracey, Newtown, Donore
William Tynan, Ballitore, 8 November
James Whyte, 24 November

LIST OF DANGEROUS MEN IN CUSTODY FROM COUNTY KILDARE, 1923 (SOURCE: MILITARY ARCHIVES, DUBLIN):

John Blong, Clonmore, Rathangan
James Brady, Church Street, Kilcock. Detained Gormanstown Camp
Thomas Cardwell, Beatty Park, Celbridge. Mountjoy Jail
Pat O'Carroll, Sallins Road, Naas. Newbridge Camp
John Cotter, Celbridge. Newbridge Camp
William Duffy, Monasterevin. Mountjoy Jail
Richard Dunne, Greenhills, Kill. Gormanstown Camp
Richard Fitzgerald, Suncroft
Augustine Fitzpatrick, Railway View, Naas. Newbridge Camp
Val Grady, Claregate Street, Kildare
Reginald Griffin, Monasterevin
Walter Halligan, Railway Bridge, Naas. Newbridge Camp
Maurice Lambe, Kilcullen. Newbridge Camp

Appendix I

Joe Martin, Old Grange, Monasterevin. Newbridge Camp
Patrick Martin, do.
Christopher Mills, Killeenmore, Kill. Gormanstown Camp
Patrick Mullaney, Leixlip. Mountjoy Jail
Michael Murphy, Maynooth Road, Celbridge. Mountjoy Jail
Thomas Murphy, Landenstown, Sallins
Patrick Neligan, Monasterevin. Newbridge Camp
Arthur O'Connor, Elm Hall, Celbridge. Mountjoy Jail
John O'Connor, Elm Hall, Celbridge. Mountjoy Jail
Michael O'Kelly, Gleann na Greine, Naas. Newbridge Camp
Michael O'Neill, Weston Park, Leixlip. Mountjoy Jail
Seán Rafferty, Basin Street, Naas. Newbridge Camp
Joseph Ryan, Brackna, Rathangan
Michael Sheehan, Main Street, Newbridge. Newbridge Camp
Patrick Sheehan, Main Street, Newbridge. Newbridge Camp
Michael Tracey, Newtown, Donore
Timothy Tyrell, Maynooth. Mountjoy Jail
Liam Tynan, Ballybrittas. Tintown, Curragh Camp
Edward Vaughan, Baronrath, Straffan. Mountjoy Jail

List of women prisoners from County Kildare in Kilmainham, Mountjoy and the North Dublin Union (source: Sinead McCoole, *No Ordinary Women*, pp. 218–38):

Brigid Barnewall, Lyons Cottages, Straffan Road, Maynooth
Peg Daly, Claregate Street, Kildare. Transferred to Mountjoy 5 March 1923
Peg Delaney, Station Road, Kildare
E. Masterson, Newbridge
Annie Moore, Rathbride
Lily Wallace, Newbridge

List of County Kildare prisoners, sentenced and unsentenced (source: *Kildare Observer*, 19 April 1924):

'Sinn Féin' contains a long list of prisoners (over 1,000) who are held in the Free State, Northern Ireland and Great Britain. Particulars relating to County Kildare men are: Thomas Cardwell, Celbridge; Jas. Dempsey, Castletown Lodge, Celbridge; Patrick Mullaney, Leixlip (formerly death sentence); Seán O'Connor, Elm Hall, Celbridge; Michael O'Neill, Weston Park, Leixlip (formerly death sentence); and Timothy Tyrell, Maynooth (formerly death sentence), all sentenced to seven years' penal servitude; and unsentenced:

In Hare Park camp: J. Brady, Church St, Kilcock; P. O'Carroll, Sallins Road, Naas; John Cotter, Celbridge; Wm. Duffy, Monasterevin; R. Fitzgerald, Feerad, Suncroft; A. Fitzpatrick, Railway View, Naas; Joseph Martin, Monasterevin; C. Mills, Painstown; Michael Murphy, Celbridge; Thomas Murphy, Landenstown, Sallins; P. Nelligan, Monasterevin; and Ed. Tracey, Newtown, Naas.

In Tintown No. 2: P. Brady, Ballymakealy, Celbridge; Peter Gill, Naas; Michael Nolan, Spratstown, Colbinstown; and P. Woods, Furryhill, Rathmore.

Appendix II

Claims for Damages in County Kildare
(Source: *Kildare Observer*, 29 July 1922)

The following malicious injury claims have been received by Kildare County Council within the past three months:

J. P. Cusack, Blackwood, Robertstown, house, etc., destroyed	£1,000
Edward Heffernan, Kildare, wall damaged	£20
A. M. O'Brien, Edenderry, goods taken from shop at Kilmeague	£20
Anthony Reeves, Gallowshill, Athy, window-breaking	£6
John Kenna, Cloneygath, Monasterevin, shed, etc., burned	£50
James Hickey, Newtown, Bert, Athy, turf burned	£35
John Jackson, Fairview, Dunlavin, motor car, etc., burned	£60
T. J. O'Neill, huts destroyed at Curragh	£415
A. W. Maloney, house, etc., damaged at Curragh	£70
Earl of Mayo, cattle driving at Rathgorrah	£25
Same, cattle shot and killed	£45
Countess of Mayo, cottage damaged at Kill	£50
W. K. Merlchan, Sherriff Hill, Moone, cottage burned	£500
M. J. Byrne, Coolree, Robertstown, cattle driven	£65
C. A. Bury, Downings, Prosperous, cattle driven	£190
Mary Quinn, Rathmore, Carbury, grass burned	£10
T. J. O'Neill, huts destroyed on Curragh	£50
Ed. Condell, Russellstown, Athy, house burned	£1,000

Duthie, Large & Co., motor car taken at Booleigh, a week, consequential damage	£270
Mary Quinn, Ticknevin, Carbury, turf destroyed	£75
R. W. Ireland, Courtduff, Donadea, cattle driving	£63
S. E. Holmes, Monasterevin, machinery removed	£350
Ernest Northern, Connaught Lodge, Kildare, house burned	£1,000
Richd Price, Grangeclare East, Carbury, tools and hay destroyed	£90
Bernard Ivers, Parsonstown, Carbury, cattle driving	£210
G. S. & G. Railway Co., goods taken at Sallins	£50
A. J. Hanbridge, Silliott Hill, Kildare, house burned	£700
Mrs C. Patrickson, Curragh, personal injury at Crotanstown	£250
Mary Quinn, Ticknevin, Carbury, boycott notice	£200
Same, fence destroyed	£30
T. H. Curtis, hay destroyed at Newbridge	£27 5s. 4d.
Helen Carew, Parsonstown, Carbury, gate destroyed	£35
Bernard Ivors, Parsonstown, Carbury, cattle driving	£144
F. L. Casey, Connaught Lodge, furniture destroyed	£115
Lord Cloncurry, barn and store destroyed at Fanagh	£120
Mrs C. Potterton, Ardkill, Carbury, cottage destroyed	£300
Navy, Army and Air Force Institute, Ford motor van destroyed at Newbridge	£120
G. S. & W. Railway Co., wagon and straw destroyed at Kildare	£350
Same, wagon and hay destroyed at Newbridge	£750
George Graham, Kildare, motor car destroyed	£190
Margaret Chaplin, Kildare, house destroyed	£450
G. S. & W. Railway Co., Baltinglass, hay seed destroyed	£200
Peter Breen, Kill, motor car taken	£350
J. S. Bird, Curragh motor car taken	£600
G. S. & W. Railway Co., grass seeds removed, Baltinglass	£60

Appendix II

The following claims relate to outrages since the commencement of the present hostilities:

June 23 – W. H. James, motor cycle taken at Ballysax	£30
June 30 – Frank Burke, Kildare, motor car taken	£500
June 28 – G. S. & W. Railway Co., railway line damaged at Moortown	£35
June 28 – Same, do. Curragh	£35
June 29 – Same, railway bridge damaged, Curragh	£150
June 28 – Same, railway line damaged, Barrettstown	£30
June 29 – Same, do. Kildangan	£150
June 29 – Same, railway bridge damaged, Kylebeg	£150
June 28 – Same, railway line damaged at Common	£60
June 27 – Dr Jas. A. McKenna, Monasterevin, motor car taken	£400
June 28 – T. Gisborne Gordon, Sunnyhill, Kilcullen, motor car taken	£700
June 16 – William White, Blackrath, dwelling house burned	£240
June 10 – A. J. Hanbridge, Silliott Hill, property burned	£100
July 4 – Maurice Higgins, Landenstown, dwelling burned	£300
July 4 – Grand Canal Co., canal bridge damaged Clogheen	£300
July 4 – Mrs Moore, Mountarmstrong, goods taken from shop	£50
July 1 – Grand Canal Co., bridge damaged at Clogheen	£1,000
July 7 – Lord Mayo, house damaged at Kill	£500
July 7 – Mrs Moore, Mountarmstrong, lambs taken at Clonkeeran	£5
July 6 – Peter Moore, Mountarmstrong, shotgun taken	£21
July 3 – Same, furniture, etc., damaged	£100
July 7 – Elizabeth & Patk Connolly, property damaged at Kildare	£30

July 7 – Jas. A. Parsons, Blessington, house, goods, etc., damaged	£150
July 3 – M. G. W. Railway Co. railway line damaged at Blakestown	£12
July 3 – Same, railway line damaged at Maynooth	£20
July 9 – Lord Cloncurry, trees, etc., destroyed at Ballyvoneen	£20
July 11 – D. C. Baird, house damaged, Manor Kilbride	£260
July 3 – Grand Canal Co. property damaged at Monasterevin	£100
July 8 – John Keogh, Ballymore-Eustace, house injured	£5,000
July 9 – T. P. Le Fanu and Earl of Drogheda, House destroyed, Monasterevin	£3,000
July 4 – G. S. & W. R. Co., line damaged at Elm Hall	£25
July 10 – Same, line damaged at Oghill	£500
July 8 – Same, bridge damaged at Passlands	£258
July 1 – Same, line damaged at Dangan	£250
July 4 – S. R. Boothman, beast killed at Tipperkevin	£24
July 3 – P. J. Weymes, house destroyed at Portarlington (Imperial Hotel)	£12,000
July 14 – G. S. & W. R. Co., apparatus damaged at Kildare	£140
July 6 – Daniel Buckley and others, house damaged at Maynooth	£50
July 15 – Grand Canal Co., bridge damaged at Rathangan	£150
July 3 – G. J. F. Verschoyle, farmhouse burned at Kilberry	£400
July 3 – James Mangan, Ford car removed at Monasterevin	£100
July 14 – G. S. & W. R. Co., line damaged at Ballylea, Colbinstown	£65
July 8 – Same, do., at Oghill	£25
July 1 – Same, bridge damaged at Toberorymore	£175
July 13 – Same, do., at Oghill	£250
July 17 – Same, do., at Yomanstown	£350

July 17 – Same, river bridge damaged at Killeenmore £350
July 18 – Same, signal cabin burned at Straffan £1,000

This leaves a total of claims received since the middle of April to the end of June £10,704, and for the three weeks from the outbreak of civil war to 18 July £25,200, or a total for three months of £35,964.

Kildare's Burden
(Source: *Kildare Observer*, 13 January 1923)

Malicious injury claims since the outbreak of the present hostilities in June. The total of claims for malicious injuries received by the Kildare County Council reaches the enormous figure of £104,453 14s 9d. None of these claims have been heard. The claims received since the end of September last total £47,465. They include the following:

G. S. & W. Railway – Cherryville bridge destroyed	£2,000
Same – Bridge wall damaged at Common	£10
Same – Oghill bridge destroyed	£2,000
Same – Property burned at Kildangan	£2,500
Same – Ballylea signal cabin damaged	£50
Same – Harristown signal cabin, etc., burned	£1,500
Same – Killeenmore bridge damaged by explosives	£100
Same – Railway wagons derailed at Athy	£12
Same – Kildare bridge and 9 wagons damaged	£1,250
Same – Cherryville railway crossing damaged	£110
Same – Clownings instruments broken, etc.	£120
Same – Oghill, cement, etc., removed	£55
Same – Kildare, instruments destroyed	£15
Same – Telephone hut damaged at Curragh	£20
Same – Engine derailed at Cherryville	£460

Same – Bridge damaged at Cush	£200
Same – Bridge No. 56 damaged by fire at Newtownpillsworth	£50
Same – Train damaged by bullets at Pollardstown (28 Nov.)	£15
Total claims by G. S. W. R. Co.	£10,467
The M. G. W. Railway Co. claims are:	
Signal cabin burned at Greenfield, Maynooth	£1,200
Permanent way damaged at railpark, Maynooth	£35
Leixlip, bridge damaged by explosives	£450
Total claims by M. G. W. R. Co.	£1,685
Other claims included are:	
B. Rock, Alasty, Kill – Hay and shed burned	£600
W. F. Hendy – Hay burned at Rickardstown	£500
A. W. Henderson, Ballitore – Binder burned	£55
Mrs E. Kehoe, Kilcoo, Athy – Hay burned	£150
J. McTiernan, Edenderry – Gate and hay destroyed	£50
T. Cullen – House and furniture burned at Rathmuck	£2,000
T. Cullen – Houses and stables burned at Doneany	£2,000
John Behan – Hay burned at Kilnagornan	£90
John Owens – Crops injured at Ballycullane	£26
Martin Lyons – Hay burned at Barrowhouse	£916
J. A. Parsons – Property damaged at Blessington	£300
W. Coleborn, Dunlavin – Ford car, petrol, etc., taken	£84 14s.
Agnes Fleming – Property seized	£58 11s.
J. J. Murphy – Clothing seized	£79 16s. 8d.
S. O'Brien, Nurney – Property seized	£17 9s. 4d.
Nicholls Carroll – Property burned at Rathmuck	£15
Mrs E. Jackson – Shed, etc., burned at Maudlins	£72

Appendix II

W. Fox – Hay burned at Maudlins	£15
Mary Brien, Monread – Hay, straw, etc., burned	£110 15s.
P. McEvoy and Sons – Bacon seized at Straffan	£11 6s.
M. Gray – Hay, etc., burned at Ballinree	£257
B. Harold – Hay burned at Baltreacey	£10
James Salter – Property seized at Blackford	£67
W. Lawlor – Goods seized at Straffan	£18 6s.
J. F. Tuthill – Barracks burned at Bannagroe	£1,000
A. Crosbie, Hodgestown – Straw, etc., burned	£80
Anne Kelly – Barley, oats, etc., burned at Clonbrown	£40
J. Nevitt, Kilmeague – Hay burned	£240
W. Lawlor – Stout taken at Umeras	£9 6s.
Imperial Tobacco Co. – Cigarettes stolen at Straffan	£34 11s. 11d.
P. Berney, Silliothill – Hay burned	£40 1s.
James Dixon, Milltown, Dunlavin – Hay, etc., burned	£2,000
J. Davis – Clothing seized at Umeras	£32
J. J. Byrne, Kilcullen – Shop window broken	£30
Mrs Margaret Donnelly – House burned at Ladytown	£5,000
F. F. MacCabe, Osborne Lodge – Fire	£500
J. A. Burke – Household goods destroyed at Ladytown	£800
S. O'Brien – Money, goods taken	£13 10s. 8d.
Commissioners of Woods and Forests – House destroyed at Curragh	£3,000
Miss C. M. Aylmer, Donadea Castle – Hay, etc. burned	£1,900
Mrs L. Cary-Barnard – Lady maimed at Commons, Hazelhatch	£5,000
Mrs E. M. Heydon, Brownstown, Athy – hay burned	£400
F. Steadman, Levitstown, Athy – Personal injuries by shooting	£500
Capt. de C. Wheeler – Damage to Robertstown courthouse	£120

Same – House damaged at Robertstown £270
Same – Robertstown police barracks damaged £120
J. J. Murphy, Kellaville, Athy – Hay burned £251
Michael Moore, Ballyfoyle, Athy – House burned £206
J. J. Bergin, Maybrook, Athy – Hay burned £80
Michael Mara, Athy – Hay burned at Shean £165
Thomas Roche, Usk, Dunlavin – Straw burned £70
F. V. Plewman, Athy – Hay burned £140

[spellings and place names retained as in original report]

Notes

INTRODUCTION

1. Campbell, C., *Emergency Law in Ireland 1918–1925* (Oxford 1994), p. 149; Kissane, B., *The Politics of the Irish Civil War* (Oxford 2005), p. 85.

1. KILDARE AT WAR: 1916–21

1. Chambers, L., *Rebellion in Kildare* (Dublin 1998), pp. 119, 122.
2. Hopkinson, M., *The Irish War of Independence* (Dublin 2002), p. 145.
3. Ferriter, D., *The Transformation of Ireland 1900–2000* (London 2005), p. 235.
4. Dooley, T., 'IRA activity in Kildare during the War of Independence', in Nolan, W. and McGrath, T. (eds), *Kildare: History and Society* (Dublin 2006), p. 641.
5. Durney, J., *On the One Road. Political Unrest in Kildare 1913–94* (Naas 2001), p. 12.
6. *Ibid.*, p. 14.
7. *Ibid.*, p. 18.
8. *Ibid.*, pp. 22, 26.
9. Interview with Karel Kiely, Kildare Genealogy Department, Newbridge, County Kildare, 1 April 2008.
10. Durney (2001), *op. cit.*, p. 32.
11. O'Mahony, S., *Frongoch: University of Revolution* (Dublin 1987), p. 205.
12. Durney (2001), *op. cit.*, p. 41.
13. *Ibid.*, p. 42.
14. *Kildare Observer*, 7 December 1918.
15. Durney (2001), *op. cit.*, p. 64.
16. Smyth, Michael, 'Kildare Battalions – 1920', *Capuchin Annual* (Dublin 1970), p. 564.
17. *Ibid.*, pp. 564–73.
18. Durney (2001), *op. cit.*, p. 61.
19. Interview with the late Paddy Sheehan, Newbridge, 2 August 2001.
20. Colgan, J., 'Leixlip Chronology 1900–2002, County Kildare', *County Kildare Online*

Electronic Historical Journal, available from: www.kildare.ie/library/ehistory, accessed 24 November 2007.
21. Durney (2001), *op. cit.*, p. 197.
22. Jim Dunne, Witness Statement (W/S) 1571, Military Archives, Cathal Brugha Barracks, Dublin. Copy in Local Studies, Genealogy and Archives Department, Newbridge Library.
23. Durney (2001), *op. cit.*, p. 197.
24. Dooley (2006), *op. cit.*, p. 635.
25. O'Keefe, P., 'My reminiscences of 1914–1923', *Oughterany, Journal of the Donadea Local History Group* (1993), vol. 1, no. 1, p. 43.
26. *Leinster Leader*, 15 January 1921.
27. Kavanagh, Seán, 'The Irish Volunteer Intelligence Organisation', *Capuchin Annual* (1969), p. 357.
28. *Ibid.*, p. 357.
29. *Ibid.*, pp. 358–63.
30. Dooley (2006), *op. cit.*, p. 650.

2. EVACUATION

1. Litton, H., *The Irish Civil War: An Illustrated History* (Dublin 1995), pp. 25–7.
2. *Ibid.*, p. 28.
3. 'Whyte's Catalogue, November 2010'. Copy in Local Studies, Genealogy and Archives Department, Newbridge Library, County Kildare.
4. *Kildare Observer*, 28 January 1922.
5. Doherty, J. E. and Hickey, D. J., *A Chronology of Irish History Since 1500* (Dublin 1989), p. 200.
6. Ferriter, D., *The Transformation of Ireland 1900–2000* (London 2005), p. 249.
7. Costello, C., *A Most Delightful Station: The British Army on the Curragh of Kildare, Ireland, 1855–1922* (Cork 1996), pp. 22–5.
8. Gibson, W. H. and Nolan, P. F., 'The military influence on Kildare towns', *The Nationalist and Leinster Times*, centenary issue 1883–1983.
9. *Kildare Observer*, 11 February 1922.
10. *Ibid.*
11. Gibson (1983), *op. cit.*
12. *Kildare Observer*, 4 March 1922.
13. *Ibid.*, 25 March 1922.
14. *Ibid.*
15. Costello (1996), *op. cit.*, pp. 336–8.

16. *Kildare Observer*, 1 April 1922.
17. *Leinster Leader*, 14 December 1985.
18. *Ibid.*, 11 June 1998.
19. *Ibid.*, 20 May 1922; Paddy Sheehan, interview in *Leinster Leader*, 8 August 1996.
20. *Leinster Leader*, 20 May 1922.
21. *Kildare Observer*, 20 May 1922.
22. Costello (1996), *op. cit.*, pp. 340–2.

3. THE KILLING OF LIEUTENANT WOGAN BROWNE

1. *The Irish Times*, 2 February 1922 and 13 February 1922.
2. Costello, C., *A Most Delightful Station: The British Army on the Curragh of Kildare, Ireland, 1855–1922* (Cork 1996), p. 331.
3. *The Irish Times*, 18 February 1922.
4. 'Obituary, Colonel Francis Wogan Browne', *The Clongownian*, June 1927, vol. XI, no. 2, pp. 103–4.
5. *Kildare Observer*, 18 February 1922.
6. *The Irish Times*, 18 February 1922.
7. *Kildare Observer*, 18 February 1922.
8. Interview with Pat Sheehan, 12 February 2001.
9. *Kildare Observer*, 18 February 1922.
10. *The Clongownian*, *op. cit.*, pp. 103–4.
11. 'Inquest on John Wogan Browne', 11 February 1922. Copy in Local Studies, Genealogy and Archives Department, Newbridge Library, County Kildare.
12. Costello (1996), *op. cit.*, pp. 332, 329.
13. *Kildare Observer*, 1 April 1922.
14. *Ibid.*, 13 December 1924.
15. *Ibid.*, 29 July 1922 and 14 April 1922.
16. *Ibid.*, 29 April 1922.
17. *Leinster Leader*, 11 March 1922.
18. *Kildare Observer*, 8 July 1922.
19. Jim Dunne, W/S 1571, Military Archives, Cathal Brugha Barracks, Dublin.

4. THE KILDARE MUTINY

1. Kenny, L., 'The Kildare mutiny recalled,' *Leinster Leader*, 21 August 1987.
2. Garvan, T., *1922: The Birth of Irish Democracy* (Dublin 1996), p. 108.
3. Allen, G., *The Garda Síochána. Policing Independent Ireland 1922–82* (Dublin 1999), p. 31.

4. Costello, C., 'Establishing the Garda', *Leinster Leader*, 25 November 1999.
5. *Irish Independent*, 7 March 1922.
6. Garvan (1996), *op. cit.*, p. 107.
7. McNiffe, L., *A History of the Garda Síochána* (Dublin 1997), p. 18.
8. *Ibid.*, p. 19.
9. Costello, C., 'Mutiny in Kildare', *Leinster Leader*, 6 March 1997.
10. John McFaul, interview in the *Leinster Leader*, 25 August 1973.
11. Brady, C., *Guardians of the Peace* (Dublin 1974), p. 53.
12. *Ibid.*, p. 53.
13. McLoughlin, M., 'The Civic Guards and the Kildare mutiny,' in Corrigan, M. (ed.), *Druim Criaig: The Ridge of Clay. A Contribution to the History of Kildare Town* (Kildare 2009), p. 80; McNiffe (1997), *op. cit.*, p. 17.
14. *Kildare Observer*, 23 April 1922.
15. McNiffe (1997), *op. cit.*, pp. 17, 36.
16. Brady (1974), *op. cit.*, pp 53–5.
17. *Kildare Observer*, 18 April 1922.
18. Allen (1999), *op. cit.*, p. 32.
19. Brady (1974), *op. cit.*, p. 56.
20. *Ibid.*, p. 56.
21. Allen (1999), *op. cit.*, p. 34.
22. McNiffe (1997), *op. cit.*, p. 19.
23. Allen (1999), *op. cit.*, p. 38.
24. Brady (1974), *op. cit.*, p. 60.
25. Kenny (1987), *op. cit.*
26. McNiffe (1997), *op. cit.*, p. 19.
27. Allen (1999), *op. cit.*, p. 39.
28. *Ibid.*, p. 40.
29. McNiffe (1997), *op. cit.*, p. 21.
30. Kenny (1987), *op. cit.*
31. McLoughlin (2009), *op. cit.*, p. 81.
32. McNiffe (1997), *op. cit.*, p. 21.
33. *Kildare Observer*, 5 August 1922.
34. McNiffe (1997), *op. cit.*, p. 21.
35. Allen (1999), *op. cit.*, p. 46.
36. McNiffe (1997), *op. cit.*, p. 24.
37. *Ibid.*, p. 27.
38. *Kildare Observer*, 30 September 1922.
39. *Leinster Leader*, 21 January 1989.

40. The Garda Síochána (Temporary Provisions) Act 1923, available from: www.irishstatutebooks.ie/1923, accessed 11 February 2010; Brady (1974), *op. cit.*, p. 128.
41. Allen (1999), *op. cit.*, p. 71.
42. *Ibid.*, p. 50.
43. *Ibid.*, p. 57.
44. *Ibid.*, p. 72.
45. Costello (1997), *op. cit.*

5. THE SPLIT

1. Hopkinson, M., *Green against Green. The Irish Civil War* (Dublin 1988), p. 61.
2. Litton, H., *The Irish Civil War: An Illustrated History* (Dublin 1995), p. 42; Hopkinson (1988), *op. cit.*, p. 61.
3. *Kildare Observer*, 7 January 1922 and 21 January 1922.
4. Garvan, T., *The Evolution of Irish Nationalist Politics* (Dublin 2005), p. 144.
5. *Kildare Observer*, 21 January 1922.
6. *Leinster Leader*, 7 April 1922.
7. Joe Buckley, Maynooth, statement in Maynooth public library.
8. Jim Dunne, W/S 1571, Military Archives, Cathal Brugha Barracks, Dublin.
9. Patrick Carroll, W/S 1161, Military Archives, Cathal Brugha Barracks, Dublin.
10. Coogan, T. P., *Michael Collins* (London 1990), p. 314; Litton (1995), *op. cit.*, p. 45; Hopkinson (1988), *op. cit.*, p. 66.
11. *Leinster Leader*, 15 April 1922.
12. Ferriter, D., *The Transformation of Ireland 1900–2000* (London 2005), p. 252.
13. *Kildare Observer*, 22 April 1922.
14. *Ibid.*
15. *Ibid.*
16. *Ibid.*
17. *Leinster Leader*, 22 April 1922.
18. *Kildare Observer*, 22 April 1922.
19. Father P. J. Doyle, W/S 807, Military Archives, Cathal Brugha Barracks, Dublin.
20. Ferriter (2005), *op. cit.*, p. 252.
21. *Leinster Leader*, 10 June 1922.
22. Coogan (1990), *op. cit.*, p. 382.
23. Tomas McSherrigh, interview, 4 January 2001.
24. Litton (1995), *op. cit.*, p. 49.
25. *Ibid.*, p. 68.
26. *Kildare Observer*, 24 June 1922.
27. *Ibid.*, 3 June 1922.

28. *The Irish Times*, 24 June 1922.
29. *Kildare Observer*, 24 June 1922.
30. Coogan (1990), *op. cit.*, p. 330.
31. *Ibid.*, p. 329.
32. *Kildare Observer*, 1 July 1922.

6. CIVIL WAR

1. *Leinster Leader*, 22 September 1979.
2. Neeson, E., *The Civil War in Ireland* (Cork 1966), p. 82.
3. Paddy Sheehan, interview with author, 2–5 February 2001.
4. *Leinster Leader*, 26 November 1977.
5. Coogan, T. P., *Michael Collins* (London 1990), p. 386.
6. *Ibid.*, p. 387.
7. *Kildare Observer*, 8 July 1922.
8. Coogan (1990), *op. cit.*, p. 382.
9. *Kildare Observer*, 8 July 1922.
10. *Ibid.*, 15 July 1922.
11. Jim Dunne, W/S 1571, Military Archives, Cathal Brugha Barracks, Dublin.
12. Hopkinson M., *Green against Green. The Irish Civil War* (Dublin 1988), pp. 70–1, 123–5.
13. Jim Dunne, W/S 1571.
14. O'Malley, E., *The Singing Flame* (Dublin 1978), p. 130.
15. *Kildare Observer*, 15 July 1922; Neeson (1966), *op. cit.*, p. 85.
16. *Leinster Leader*, 17 July 1997.
17. *Kildare Observer*, 8 July 1922.
18. *Ibid.*; Neeson (1966), *op. cit.*, p. 86.
19. *Kildare Observer*, 8 July 1922.
20. Jim Dunne, W/S 1571.
21. *Leinster Leader*, 15 July 1922.
22. *Kildare Observer*, 15 July 1922.
23. *Leinster Leader*, 8 July 1961.
24. *Ibid.*
25. Durney, J., *On the One Road. Political Unrest in Kildare 1913–94* (Naas 2001), p. 115.
26. O'Malley (1978), *op. cit.*, p. 133.
27. Costello C., *A Class Apart. The Gentry Families of County Kildare* (Dublin 2005), p. 121.

28. Jim Dunne, W/S 1571; *Kildare Observer*, 15 July 1922.
29. Pat Sheehan, interview with author, 2–5 February 2001; Jim Dunne W/S 1571; *Kildare Observer*, 15 July 1922.
30. *Kildare Observer*, 22 July 1922.
31. Durney (2001), *op. cit.*, p. 116.
32. Interview with Frank Lawler, 30 August 2007.
33. *Leinster Leader*, 2 October 1972.
34. Meda Ryan, *The Day Michael Collins Was Shot* (Dublin 1989), p. 36.
35. *Leinster Leader*, 19 August 1922.
36. As related to James Durney by his great-aunt Ellen Gaul, Naas, *c.* 1978.
37. *Ibid.*, p. 117.
38. Father P. J. Doyle, W/S 807, Military Archives, Cathal Brugha Barracks, Dublin.
39. *Ibid.*
40. *Ibid.*

7. GUERRILLA DAYS IN KILDARE

1. Hopkinson M., *Green against Green. The Irish Civil War* (Dublin 1988), p. 170.
2. O'Keefe, P., 'My reminiscences of 1914–1923', *Oughterany, Journal of the Donadea Local History Group* (1993), vol. 1, no. 1, p. 48.
3. Jim Dunne, W/S 1571, Military Archives, Cathal Brugha Barracks, Dublin.
4. Interview with Art McCoy, 9 April 2008.
5. Hopkinson (1988), *op. cit.*, p. 182.
6. National Graves Association, *The Last Post. The Details and Stories of Republican Dead 1913/1975* (Dublin 1976), p. 97; Jim Dunne, W/S 1571.
7. *Kildare Observer*, 23 September 1922.
8. Coogan, T. P., *Ireland in the Twentieth Century* (London 2003), p. 138.
9. Jim Dunne, W/S 1571.
10. *Kildare Observer*, 21 October 1922.
11. *Ibid.*
12. 'Report of inquest at the workhouse, Carlow, 25 October 1922'. Copy in Local Studies, Genealogy and Archives Department, Newbridge Library.
13. *Ibid.*
14. *Kildare Observer*, 21 October 1922.
15. *Ibid.*
16. *Ibid.*, 4 November 1922.
17. *Ibid.*, 2 December 1922.
18. Jim Dunne, W/S 1571.

19. *Kildare Observer*, 21 October 1992, 28 October 1922, 25 November 1922 and 9 December 1922.
20. Keane, V., 'The Leixlip Column'. Copy in Local Studies, Genealogy and Archives Department, Newbridge Library.
21. Cummins, S., 'A shout in the night. The rise and fall of the Leixlip Irregulars July–December 1922'. Copy in Local Studies, Genealogy and Archives Department, Newbridge Library.
22. *Ibid.*; Keane, *op. cit.*.
23. Report on Leixlip/Maynooth Operation, 1 December 1922, compiled by W. Frayne, brigade intelligence officer, Military Archives, Cathal Brugha Barracks, Dublin. Copy in Local Studies, Genealogy and Archives Department, Newbridge Library. Captured men of the Mullaney column: Patrick Mullaney, John O'Connor (wounded), William Wyse (wounded), Thomas Kealy (wounded), Michael O'Neill, Thomas Cardwell, Bertie Hawney, John Curley, Tim Tyrell, Francis Brennan, James Dempsey, John Gaynor, James Kelly, Charles Kelly, Thomas McCann, Patrick Nolan, Thomas O'Brien, Leo Dowling, Terence Brady, Sylvester Heany, Laurence Sheehy, Anthony O'Reilly (the last five deserted from the National Army).
24 O'Dwyer, M., '*Seventy-seven of Mine*,' *said Ireland* (Cashel 2006) p. 174.
25. *Kildare Observer*, 2 and 9 December 1922; *Leinster Leader*, 16 December 1922; O'Dwyer (2006), *op. cit.*, pp. 154–74.
26. Copy of letter in author's possession.
27. Durney, J., *On the One Road. Political Unrest in Kildare 1913–94* (Naas 2001), p. 126.
28. Cummins, *op. cit.*

8. THE GREAT ESCAPE

1. 'The escapes from Newbridge Barracks', *Leinster Leader*, 31 December 1927.
2. Durney, J., *On the One Road. Political Unrest in Kildare 1913–94* (Naas 2001), p. 119.
3. *Leinster Leader*, 31 December 1927.
4. O'Keefe, P., 'My reminiscences of 1914–1923', *Oughterany, Journal of the Donadea Local History Group* (1993), vol. 1, no. 1.
5. *Leinster Leader*, 31 December 1927.
6. Mick Sheehan, interview with Ann Donohue, 1989, local history project. Copy in Local Studies, Genealogy and Archives Department, Newbridge Library.
7. *Leinster Leader*, 31 December 1927.
8. Sheehan–Donohue interview, *op. cit.*
9. *Leinster Leader*, 31 December 1927.
10. *Kildare Observer*, 21 October 1922.

11. Sheehan–Donohue interview, *op. cit.*
12. Paddy Sheehan interview with author, 10/11 March 2001.
13. *Leinster Leader*, 31 December 1927.
14. *Ibid.*
15. *Kildare Observer*, 21 October 1922.
16. *Leinster Leader*, 21 October 1922.
17. Jim Dunne, W/S 1571, Military Archives, Cathal Brugha Barracks, Dublin.
18. *Kildare Observer*, 15 July 1922.
19. J. White obituary, *Leinster Leader*, 10 February 1973.
20. James Pooge (relative of Jimmy Whyte), correspondence with author, 6 August 2009.
21. Sheehan–Donohue interview, *op. cit.*
22. Durney (2001), *op. cit.*, p. 122.
23. *Kildare Observer*, 21 October 1922.
24. Andrews, C. S., *Dublin Made Me* (Dublin 1979), p. 294.
25. Durney (2001), *op. cit.*, p. 127.
26. Curran, J. M., *The Birth of the Irish Free State 1921–1923* (Alabama 1980), p. 264.
27. *Ibid.*, p. 265.
28. Campbell, C., *Emergency Law in Ireland 1918–1925* (Oxford 1994), p. 97.

9. 'SEVEN OF MINE,' SAID IRELAND

1. Jim Dunne, W/S 1571, Military Archives, Cathal Brugha Barracks, Dublin.
2. Data on 'Rathbride Column', untitled box number, Civil War Collection, Military Archives, Dublin.
3. Colm McEvoy, family papers, copy in Local Studies, Genealogy and Archives Department, Newbridge Library.
4. *Kildare Observer*, 16 December 1922.
5. *Ibid.*, 19 November 1922.
6. *Ibid.*, 21 October 1922.
7. *Leinster Leader*, 16 December 1922; John O'Reilly, correspondence with author, 9 April 2010.
8. Interview with Marie Maher, 7 March 2001; O'Reilly correspondence with author (2010).
9. *Leinster Leader*, 23 December 1922.
10. Sheehan interview 2001, author; Maher interview 2001, author.
11. *Leinster Leader*, 23 December 1922.
12. Mullowney, A. J., 'Executions – 1922', unpublished lecture. Copy in Local Studies, Genealogy and Archives Department, Newbridge Library.

13. O'Dwyer, M., *'Seventy-seven of Mine,' said Ireland* (Cashel 2006), p. 120.
14. Copy of letters in author's possession.
15. *Éire. The Irish Nation*, 31 March 1923.
16. McCoole, S., *No Ordinary Women. Irish Female Activists in the Revolutionary Years 1900–1923* (Dublin 2003), p. 130.
17. Sheehan interview 2001, author; Jim Dunne, W/S 1571.
18. Jim Dunne, W/S 1571.
19. *Leinster Leader*, 23 December 1922.

10. YOUTHFUL INCENDIARIES

1. Dooley, T., *The Decline of the Big House in Ireland* (Dublin 2001), p. 287.
2. Statistics taken from compensation claims in *Kildare Observer* (see also Appendix II).
3. Dooley (2001), *op. cit.*, p. 187.
4. *Kildare Observer*, 2 December 1922.
5. Dooley (2001), *op. cit.*, pp. 188–90.
6. Costello, C., 'Palmerstown and the Bourkes', *Leinster Leader*, 2 April 1985.
7. *Leinster Leader*, 7 January 1928.
8. *Ibid.*
9. *Ibid.*, 12 December 1925.
10. *Ibid.*
11. *Ibid.*
12. Dooley (2001), *op. cit.*, p. 174.
13. *Ibid.*
14. Costello (1985), *op. cit.*
15. Costello, C., *A Class Apart. The Gentry Families of County Kildare* (Dublin 2005), p. 76.
16. Dooley (2001), *op. cit.*, p. 197.
17. *Leinster Leader*, 12 December 1925.
18. Costello (2005), *op. cit.*, p. 107.
19. *Ibid.*, p. 86.
20. *Kildare Observer*, 17 March 1923.

11. TINTOWN

1. Crawford, H. 'The internment camps', in McLoughlin, M. (ed.), *The Curragh Revisited*, Curragh Local History Group (Curragh 2002), p. 10.
2. *Ibid.*, p. 10; Costello, C., 'Internment on the Curragh', *Leinster Leader*, 5 June 1997.

3. *Kildare Observer*, 15 July 1922.
4. Crawford (2002), *op. cit.*, p. 10.
5. Campbell, C., *Emergency Law in Ireland 1918–1925* (Oxford 1994), pp. 179, 227.
6. *Ibid.*, p. 226.
7. Maguire, J., *IRA Internments and the Irish Government. Subversives and the State 1939–1962* (Dublin 2008), p. 11.
8. Questions on treatment of prisoners by Ailfrid O'Brion. Dáil Éireann debates, vol. IV, 31 October 1923, available from: http://historicaldebates.oireachtas.ie, accessed 8 April 2010.
9. *Leinster Leader*, 20 September 1922.
10. *Ibid.*
11. Display in Kilmainham Gaol, *c.* February 2001.
12. *Ibid.*
13. O'Donnell, P., *The Gates Flew Open* (London 1932), pp. 96–7.
14. *Ibid.*, pp. 96–8.
15. Durney, J., *On the One Road. Political Unrest in Kildare 1913–94* (Naas 2001), pp. 137–8.
16. O'Malley, E., *The Singing Flame* (Dublin 1978), p. 272.
17. Campbell (1994), *op. cit.*, p. 230
18. *Ibid.*
19. *Ibid.*
20. *Ibid.*
21. Maguire (2008), *op. cit.*, p. 11.
22. Doherty, J. E. and Hickey, D. J., *A Chronology of Irish History Since 1500* (Dublin 1989), p. 296.

12. PEACE COMES DROPPING SLOW

1. Casualty list, Military Archives, Cathal Brugha Barracks, Dublin.
2. *Kildare Observer*, 10 March 1923.
3. *Ibid.*, 27 January 1923.
4. Ferriter, D., *The Transformation of Ireland 1900–2000* (London 2005), p. 264; Mulcahy, R., 'Mulcahy and Collins: A fortuitous leadership', *The Irish Sword. Journal of the Military History Society of Ireland*, 2010, vol. XXVII, no. 108, p. 97.
5. Durney, J., *On the One Road. Political Unrest in Kildare 1913–94* (Naas 2001), p. 133.
6. *Kildare Observer*, 19 August 1922.
7. *Ibid.*, 31 March 1923.
8. *Ibid.*, 7 April 1923.
9. *Ibid.*, 21 April 1923.

10. Durney (2001), *op. cit.*, p. 134.
11. Neeson, E., *The Civil War in Ireland* (Cork 1966), p. 286.
12. Younger, C., *Ireland's Civil War* (London 1968), pp. 507ff.
13. *Kildare Observer*, 28 April 1923 and 15 December 1922.
14. Costello, C., 'Internment on the Curragh', *Leinster Leader*, 5 June 1997.
15. *Kildare Observer*, 19 May 1923; Costello (1997), *op. cit.*
16. Durney (2001), *op. cit.*, p. 134.
17. Estimates based on casualty list in Military Archives, Dublin and list of republican dead in National Graves Association, *The Last Post. The Details and Stories of Republican Dead 1913/1975* (1976), pp. 92–110.
18. Litton, H., *The Irish Civil War: An Illustrated History* (Dublin 1995), p. 82.
19. *Kildare Observer*, 3 March 1923.
20. Durney (2001), *op. cit.*, p. 135.
21. Art O'Connor, family file, courtesy of Seán O'Connor, Celbridge, County Kildare.

13. HUNGER STRIKE, MURDER AND MUTINY

1. Sugg, W., 'Post Civil War hunger strikes', *An Phoblacht (Republican News)*, 15 October 1998.
2. Durney, J., *On the One Road. Political Unrest in Kildare 1913–94* (Naas 2001), p. 138.
3. Sugg (1998), *op cit.*
4. *Leinster Leader*, 1 December 1923 and 2 August 1924; *The Irish Times*, 24 and 30 November 1923.
5. Hopkinson, M., *Green against Green. The Irish Civil War* (Dublin 1988), pp. 268–9.
6. Sugg (1998), *op. cit.*
7. *Éire. The Irish Nation*, 12 December 1923.
8. Andrews, C. S., *Dublin Made Me* (Dublin 1979), p. 296.
9. O'Malley, E., *The Singing Flame* (Dublin 1978), p. 290.
10. *Ibid.*
11. *Kildare Observer*, 14 June 1924.
12. Durney (2001), *op. cit.*, p. 139–40.
13. Bourke, M., 'Shooting the messenger: Colonel Costello and the Murray case', *Tipperary Historical Journal*, 1997, pp. 52–4.
14. *Ibid.*
15. Costello, C., 'Justice or injustice?', *Leinster Leader*, 29 August 1996.
16. *Leinster Leader*, 13 and 20 June 1939.
17. Costello (1996), *op. cit.*
18. *Leinster Leader*, 20 September 1939.
19. Costello (1996), *op. cit.*

20. *Leinster Leader*, 28 November 1925 and 24 April 1926.
21. Durney (2001), *op. cit.*, p. 141.
22. Corry, E., *Kildare GAA Centenary History* (Newbridge 1984), p. 130.
23. *Leinster Leader*, 16 April 1983.
24. Durney (2001), *op. cit.*, p. 136.
25. De Vere White, T., *Kevin O'Higgins* (Dublin 1986), pp. 159–61.
26. *Leinster Leader*, 10 April 1926.
27. Durney (2001), *op. cit.*, pp. 141–2.

CONCLUSION

1. Hanley, B., *The IRA 1926–1936* (Dublin 2002), p. 11.
2. Campbell, C., *Emergency Law in Ireland 1918–1925* (Oxford 1994), p. 156.
3. Neeson, E., *The Civil War in Ireland* (Cork 1966), p. 81.
4. *Ibid.*, p. 174.
5. Younger, C., *Ireland's Civil War* (London 1968), p. 497.
6. John O'Reilly (son of Annie Moore), interview/correspondence with author, 12 January and 9 April 2010.
7. O'Malley, E., *The Singing Flame* (Dublin 1978), p. 289.

Bibliography

Allen, G., *The Garda Síochána. Policing Independent Ireland 1922–82* (Dublin 1999)

Andrews, C. S., *Dublin Made Me* (Dublin 1979)

Bourke, M., 'Shooting the messenger: Colonel Costello and the Murray case', *Tipperary Historical Journal*, 1997

Brady, C., *Guardians of the Peace* (Dublin 1974)

Breen, D., *My Fight for Irish Freedom* (Dublin 1978)

Campbell, C., *Emergency Law in Ireland 1918–1925* (Oxford 1994)

Chambers, L., *Rebellion in Kildare* (Dublin 1998)

Colgan, J., 'Leixlip Chronology 1900–2002, County Kildare', *County Kildare Online Electronic Historical Journal*

Coogan, T. P., *Ireland in the Twentieth Century* (London 2003)

—— *Michael Collins* (London 1990)

Corrigan, M. (ed.), *Druim Criaig: The Ridge of Clay. A Contribution to the History of Kildare Town* (Kildare 2009)

Corry, E., *Kildare GAA Centenary History* (Newbridge 1984)

Costello, C., *A Class Apart. The Gentry Families of County Kildare* (Dublin 2005)

—— *A Most Delightful Station: The British Army on the Curragh of Kildare, Ireland, 1855–1922* (Cork 1996)

—— 'Establishing the Garda', *Leinster Leader*, 25 November 1999

—— 'Internment on the Curragh', *Leinster Leader*, 5 June 1997

—— 'Justice or injustice?', *Leinster Leader*, 29 August 1996

—— 'Mutiny in Kildare', *Leinster Leader*, 6 March 1997

—— 'Palmerstown and the Bourkes', *Leinster Leader*, 2 April 1985

Crawford, H., 'The internment camps', in McLoughlin, M. (ed.), *The*

BIBLIOGRAPHY

Curragh Revisited, Curragh Local History Group (Curragh 2002)

Cummins, S., 'A shout in the night. The rise and fall of the Leixlip Irregulars, July–December 1922'. Copy in Local Studies, Genealogy and Archives Department, Newbridge Library

Curran, J. M., *The Birth of the Irish Free State 1921–1923* (Alabama 1980)

De Vere White, T., *Kevin O'Higgins* (Dublin 1986)

Doherty, J. E. and Hickey, D. J., *A Chronology of Irish History Since 1500* (Dublin 1989)

Dooley, T., 'IRA activity in Kildare during the War of Independence', in Nolan, W. and McGrath, T. (eds), *Kildare: History and Society* (Dublin 2006)

—— *The Decline of the Big House in Ireland* (Dublin 2001)

Durney, J., *On the One Road. Political Unrest in Kildare 1913–94* (Naas 2001)

Durney, J., Corrigan, M. and Curran, S. (eds), *A Forgotten Hero: John Devoy* (Naas 2009)

Feehan, J., *Cuirreach Life. The Curragh of Kildare, Ireland* (Dublin 2008)

Ferriter, D., *The Transformation of Ireland 1900–2000* (London 2005)

Garvan, T., *1922: The Birth of Irish Democracy* (Dublin 1996)

—— *The Evolution of Irish Nationalist Politics* (Dublin 2005)

Gibson, W. H. and Nolan, P. F., 'Military influence on Kildare towns', *The Nationalist and Leinster Times*, centenary issue 1883–1983

Hanley, B., *The IRA 1926–1936* (Dublin 2002)

Hart, P., *The IRA at War 1916–1923* (Oxford 2005)

Hopkinson, M., *Green against Green. The Irish Civil War* (Dublin 1988)

—— *The Irish War of Independence* (Dublin 2002)

Kavanagh, Seán, 'The Irish Volunteer Intelligence Organisation', *Capuchin Annual* (1969)

Keane, V., 'The Leixlip Column'. Copy in Local Studies, Genealogy and Archives Department, Newbridge Library

Kenny, L., 'The Kildare mutiny recalled', *Leinster Leader*, 21 August 1987

Kissane, B., *The Politics of the Irish Civil War* (Oxford 2005)

Litton, H., *The Irish Civil War: An Illustrated History* (Dublin 1995)

Maguire, J., *IRA Internments and the Irish Government. Subversives and the State 1939–1962* (Dublin 2008)

McCoole, S., *No Ordinary Women. Irish Female Activists in the Revolutionary Years 1900–1923* (Dublin 2003)

McLoughlin, M., 'The Civic Guards and the Kildare mutiny', in Corrigan, M. (ed.), *Druim Criaig: The Ridge of Clay. A Contribution to the History of Kildare Town* (Kildare 2009)

McNiffe, L., *A History of the Garda Síochána* (Dublin 1997)

Moody, T. W., Martin, F. X. and Byrne, F. J. (eds), *A New History of Ireland*, vol. viii (Oxford 1982)

Mulcahy, R., 'Mulcahy and Collins: A fortuitous leadership', *The Irish Sword, Journal of the Military History Society of Ireland*, 2010, vol. XXVII, no. 108

Mullowney, A. J., 'Executions – 1922', unpublished lecture. Copy in Local Studies, Genealogy and Archives Department, Newbridge Library

National Graves Association, *The Last Post. The Details and Stories of Republican Dead 1913/1975* (Dublin 1976)

Neeson, E., *The Civil War in Ireland* (Cork 1966)

Nolan, W. and McGrath, T. (eds), *Kildare. History and Society* (Dublin 2005)

O'Donnell, P., *The Gates Flew Open* (London 1932)

O'Dwyer, M., *'Seventy-seven of Mine,' said Ireland* (Cashel 2006)

O'Keefe, P., 'My reminiscences of 1914–1923', *Oughterany, Journal of the Donadea Local History Group*, 1993, vol. 1, no. 1

O'Mahony, S., *Frongoch: University of Revolution* (Dublin 1987)

O'Malley, E., *The Singing Flame* (Dublin 1978)

Ryan, M., *The Day Michael Collins Was Shot* (Dublin 1989)

Rynne, S., 'The man we commemorate', in Durney, J., Corrigan, M. and Curran, S. (eds), *A Forgotten Hero: John Devoy* (Naas 2009)

Smyth, Michael, 'Kildare Battalions – 1920', *Capuchin Annual* (Dublin 1970)

Sugg, W., 'Post Civil War hunger strikes', *An Phoblacht (Republican News)*, 15 October 1998

Swan, D., *Handbook of the Curragh Command* (Curragh 1984)
Younger, C., *Ireland's Civil War* (London 1968)

INTERVIEWS

Karel Kiely, Genealogist, Kildare Genealogy Department, Newbridge, County Kildare, 1 April 2008. Found record which stated that George Geoghegan was born on the Curragh.

The late Paddy Sheehan, Henry Street, Newbridge, various dates in 2001. Pat Sheehan was a brother of internee Mick Sheehan.

The late Marie Maher, niece of Tom Behan, 7 March 2001.

Interview and correspondence with John O'Reilly, Thorpe-Bay, Southend on Sea, Essex, England, 12 January and 9 April 2010. John O'Reilly's mother, Annie Moore, was arrested at Rathbride, Kildare, on 13 December 1922.

Frank Lawlor, Naas, the son of the late Peter Lawlor, 30 August 2007.

Art McCoy, Kill, the son of the late John McCoy, 9 April 2008.

OTHER SOURCES

Dáil Éireann debates. Available from: http://historicaldebates.oireachtas.ie
Éire. The Irish Nation
An Phoblacht (Republican News)
Irish Independent
The Irish Times
Kildare Observer
Leinster Leader
The Capuchin Annual
www.kildare.ie/library/ehistory
www.Irishstatutebooks.ie/23

INDEX

1st Battalion, Kildare IRA 21, 72, 78, 84
1st Eastern Division, IRA 45, 60, 62, 81, 95, 125
2nd Battalion, Kildare 21
4th Battalion, Kildare IRA 78, 102
4th Northern Division, IRA 91
5th Battalion, Kildare IRA 93
5th Brigade, 1st Eastern Division 60
5th Dublin Battalion 123
6th Battalion, Carlow Brigade 21, 73, 172
6th Battalion, Kildare IRA 78, 79, 84, 102, 116, 122
7th Brigade, Kildare IRA 61, 97

A

Adara House 137
Aiken, Frank 9, 91, 92, 157, 161, 171
Allenwood 24
Allison, Patrick 99, 100
Andrews, C.S. 'Todd' 92, 102, 117, 166
Anglo-Irish Treaty 28, 29, 31, 36, 37, 38, 44, 58, 59, 60, 61, 62, 63, 64, 66, 68, 70, 71, 74, 77, 147, 158
Anglo-Irish war 37
Anti-Treatyites, see also Republican 57, 58, 59, 64, 69, 102, 139
An tÓglách 34, 155
Armagh 91, 94
Army Convention 59
Army Council 61, 119, 148, 155, 157, 173
Arvonia 110, 111, 116
Athgarvan 19, 20, 21

Athlone 32, 40
Athy 20, 22, 23, 34, 57, 64, 84, 98, 100, 110, 136, 154, 155, 156, 159, 165, 181, 182, 187, 191, 192, 193, 194
Auxiliaries 29
Aylward, E. 68

B

Bagnall, Patrick 122, 126, 130, 131
Bagnelstown 99
Bailey, Pte Michael 101
Baldonnel 14, 101, 102, 105, 158
Ballinadrimna 22
Ballitore 79, 94, 182, 183, 184, 192
Ballsbridge 47, 49
Ballycane 79
Ballygoran 105
Ballygoran House 105
Ballygraney 181, 182
Ballykinlar 147
Ballymacarbery 157
Ballymany 23
Ballymore-Eustace 79, 80, 143, 150, 158, 182, 183, 190
Ballysax 40, 110, 116, 189
Ballyshannon 94
Baltiboys 144
Baltinglass 83, 84, 85, 94, 98, 100, 188
Bansha 122, 126
Barnewall, Brigid 185
Barrett, Richard 119, 121
Barrowhouse 18, 23, 172, 192
Barry, Denis 163
Barry, Kevin 87
Barry, Tom 54, 69, 78, 94
Barton, Robert 28, 29, 59, 68, 70,

Index

71, 75
Béal na mBláth 88
Bean, James 181
Béaslaí, Piaras 34, 155
Beggar's Bush barracks 58, 59, 62, 69, 79, 101
Behan, James 183
Behan, Pte Peter 101
Behan, Comdt Thomas 122, 123, 125, 126
Belfast Boycott 22
Bergin, John James 70
Bergin, Joseph 167, 168, 169, 170, 171
Bishop, Comdt 79
Black and Tans 19, 23, 29, 31, 46, 49, 53, 67, 147
Blackchurch 77, 80
Blackwood 97, 136, 187
Blessington 78, 79, 80, 84, 143, 190, 192
Blong, John 184
Blythe, Ernest 119, 163
Boland, Gerry 78, 167
Boland, Harry 68, 78
Bourke, Frank 20, 110
Boylan, Col Comdt Seán 32, 62
Boyle, Owen 164
Boyle, T. 150
Bracken, Joseph 154
Bracknagh 93, 94, 134
Brady, James (Celbridge) 183
Brady, James (Kilcock) 182, 184, 186
Brady, Pte Terence 105, 106
Brannockstown 96, 181
Brennan, Daniel 77
Brennan, Fintan 74
Brennan, Paddy 77, 78, 81, 84, 93, 95, 96, 183
Brennan, Col Patrick 45, 46, 47, 52
Breslin, John 77
British/crown forces 18, 21, 22, 23, 27, 28, 29, 30, 31, 32, 33, 35, 37, 38, 42, 47, 48, 58, 69, 82, 86, 100, 109, 110, 120, 123, 138, 143, 177, 178, 179

Brittas 78, 79
Brosnan, Con 171
Brownstown 193
Broy, Eamon 25, 26, 74
Brugha, Cathal 75, 76, 78
Buachalla, Domhnall Ua 14, 20, 21, 28, 29, 59, 61, 68, 70, 76, 102
Buckley, Joe 61
Buckley, Margaret 133
Buggle, Comdt 97
Bunclody 84
Burke, John 181, 183
Butterfield, William 183
Byrne, Christopher M. 29, 64, 70, 71
Byrne, Comdt W. 78, 79, 85, 102, 110, 116
Byrne, Denis 183
Byrne, Edward 99, 100
Byrne, John 53
Byrne, Mary 100

C

Camross 167
Canal bridges 18, 20, 24, 103, 189, 190
Caragh 97, 117, 183
Carbury 20, 24, 110, 182, 184, 187, 188
Cardwell, Annie 158
Cardwell, Leo 157, 158
Cardwell, Thomas 167, 181, 184, 186
Carlow 20, 21, 48, 70, 73, 79, 83, 84, 87, 98, 99, 155, 172
Casement, Roger 47, 49
Casey, Lieutenant 80, 81
Casey, Patrick 26
Cassidy, Jack 116
Castlebrowne 39
Castledermot 21, 22, 57, 70, 83, 98, 101, 156, 159, 181, 182, 184
Castlejordan 93
Castletown House 145
Caulfield, Vol. 183
Celbridge 20, 22, 23, 24, 57, 59, 77, 92, 94, 97, 102, 106, 123, 145,

221

146, 157, 167, 181, 183, 184, 185, 186
Chaplin, Margaret 42, 188
Cherryville 124, 191
Childers, Erskine 70
Churchill, Winston 29, 38, 40, 71
Civic Guard. *See* Garda Síochána
Clane 22, 39, 57, 64, 155, 156
Cleary, James 168
Clifford, William 117, 181
Clonbullogue 171
Cloncurry, Lord 146, 188, 190
Cloney 57
Clongowes 39
Collins, James 93, 109, 171, 172, 182
Collins, Margaret 96
Collins, Michael 25, 26, 28, 29, 34, 36, 38, 39, 40, 44, 45, 46, 51, 52, 53, 59, 64, 65, 66, 67, 68, 71, 74, 79, 83, 86, 87, 88, 89, 94, 95, 111, 121, 127, 155, 177
Collinstown 103, 104, 182
Colohan, Hugh 70, 71
Colton, James 181, 184
Conlan, Frank 'Joyce' 25
Conlon, John 183
Connaught Lodge 42, 136, 188
Conroy, Andrew 183
Conway, Richard 183
Coolcarrigan House 78, 81, 84, 85
Corduff 181
Cork 13, 17, 18, 37, 42, 68, 86, 88, 89, 111, 118, 162, 163
Corry, Capt. 51
Cosgrave, W. T. 95, 119, 138, 173
Costello, Col M. J. 167, 168, 169, 170
Cotter, John 181, 184, 186
Crampton, Francis 100
Crehelp 94
Criminal Investigation Department (CID) 56, 95, 134, 135
Crinnigan, Peter 182
Cullinagh 172
Cumann na mBan 19, 34, 59, 93, 94
Curragh 14, 17, 18, 19, 20, 22, 23, 29, 30, 32, 33, 34, 35, 36, 41, 42, 50, 51, 69, 77, 79, 80, 81, 83, 84, 85, 87, 88, 94, 97, 101, 106, 117, 118, 120, 121, 122, 123, 124, 125, 127, 128, 129, 131, 132, 137, 138, 139, 140, 144, 147, 149, 150, 151, 154, 155, 157, 158, 162, 163, 164, 165, 167, 169, 171, 172, 174, 177, 178, 185, 187, 188, 189, 191, 193
Curragh Mutiny 30
Curraghtown 82
Curran, Charles 110, 183
Curran, Hugh 110, 183

D

Dáil Éireann 28, 29, 45, 46, 52, 54, 59, 60, 61, 63, 64, 68, 74, 77, 83, 95, 119, 121, 139, 161, 173
Dalton, Col Charles 173
Daly, Peg 94, 168, 185
Daly, Thomas 49, 50, 51, 53, 54
de Burgh, Capt. Charles 145
de Burgh, General Eric 146
Delaney, Peg 185
Dempsey, Jim 167, 186
Derrig, Tom 79, 85, 164, 167
de Valera, Eamon 28, 34, 52, 66, 68, 75, 77, 87, 94, 95, 157, 174
Devoy, John 171
Dineen, Comdt 79
Dominic, Fr 129
Donadea 22, 188, 193
Donnelly, Fr 127
Donnelly, James 183
Donnelly, Margaret 137, 193
Donore 184, 185
Donovan, Edward 181
Dooley, Jer 93, 134
Dooley, Pte John 101
Dooley, Sgt John 170
Doran, Thomas 77, 181
Dowdenstown 137
Dowling, Capt. 144

INDEX

Dowling, Leo 105, 106
Downey, Daniel 162
Doyle, Fr P.J. 59, 64, 65, 67, 68, 88, 89
Driver, Frank 183
Driver, T. 150
Dublin 13, 14, 17, 18, 19, 20, 31, 34, 35, 42, 44, 50, 51, 53, 54, 56, 58, 59, 63, 64, 67, 68, 69, 73, 77, 78, 79, 80, 83, 87, 89, 92, 94, 95, 96, 97, 102, 103, 110, 111, 118, 121, 123, 134, 135, 144, 158, 168, 173
Dublin Brigade 74, 77, 83, 102
Dublin Castle 17, 29, 74, 174
Dublin Guards 93, 127
Dublin Metropolitan Police (DMP) 25, 45, 56, 57, 67
Dudley, General 42
Duffy, Liam 73
Duffy, Matthew 183
Duffy, William 184, 186
Duggan, Éamonn 44, 47, 51, 52, 55
Dundalk 14, 91, 92, 93, 94, 102, 116, 162, 171
Duneany 57, 137
Dun Laoghaire 110
Dunlavin 85, 94, 150, 187, 192, 193, 194
Dunleer 92, 106
Dunne, Capt. Patrick 23
Dunne, Comdt Jim 14, 23, 24, 62, 77, 78, 81, 84, 86, 92, 94, 96, 97, 101, 102, 116, 134, 159
Dunne, Fanny 94
Dunne, May 94
Dunne, Richard 182, 184
Dunne, Thomas 'Smack' 70
Dwyer, James 64

E

Easter Rising 19, 20, 21, 25, 147
Edenderry 24, 84, 93, 94, 187, 192
Éire. The Irish Nation 128, 130, 165
Ennis, Comdt Tom 85

Enniscorthy 117
Everett, James 70, 71
Executions 14, 15, 25, 97, 106, 119, 120, 121, 122, 123, 126, 127, 128, 130, 132, 133, 134, 136, 139, 155, 158, 174, 177, 178
Executive Council (Free State) 96, 119, 153, 174

F

Fanning, Fr 64
Farmers Party 71
Farm Workers' Strike 22, 155
Farrell, Desmond 34
Fay, H. C. 65
Fianna Éireann 19, 72, 74, 88
Fingall, Lady Daisy 145
FitzAlan, Lord 43
Fitzgerald, Capt. 80
Fitzgerald, Desmond 119
Fitzgerald, J.J. 36
Fitzgerald, Richard 181, 184, 186
Fitzpatrick, Augustine (Gus) 62, 171, 181, 184
Fogarty, Fr 64
Four Courts 13, 54, 63, 68, 69, 71, 72, 73, 74, 77, 78, 118, 121
Freeman's Journal 33, 76
Free State 29, 34, 44, 56, 74, 96, 118, 119, 120, 121, 123, 124, 125, 136, 139, 143, 149, 153, 157, 159, 161, 162, 164, 172, 173, 177, 178, 186
Free State army. *See* National Army
Frongoch 20

G

Gaelic Athletic Association (GAA) 108, 171
Gaelic League 26
Gaffney, Thomas 183
Gannon, Bill 110, 171
Garda Síochána/Civic Guard 34, 40, 45, 46, 47, 48, 49, 51, 52, 53,

54, 55, 56, 57, 63, 67, 82, 134, 143, 145, 154, 156, 157, 159, 174, 175, 179
Garry, Stephen 65
Gaul, Ellen 87
Gavin, Joseph 183
General Headquarters, IRA (GHQ), civil war period 102
General Headquarters, IRA (GHQ), pre-Treaty 19, 21, 22, 23, 27, 167
General Headquarters, National Army (GHQ) 62, 126
Geoghegan, George 20
Gibbet Rath 147
Gibbons, Joe 165
Gill, Peter 181, 186
Ginnity, Matthew 162
Glasshouse, the 118, 121, 125, 126, 127, 149, 150, 167
Glenealy 70
Gormanstown 32, 110, 152, 162, 164, 182, 184, 185
GPO 20, 47
Grady, Val 184
Graham, Bertie 110
Graham, Jack 42
Granard, Lord 152
Grand Canal 167, 168, 170
Graney 98
Grangewilliam House 103, 104
Greenhills 18, 23, 94, 182, 184
Griffin, Reginald 184
Griffith, Arthur 28, 29, 52, 55, 87

H

Haccius, R.A. 152
Hade, Phil 77
Hales, Seán 119, 121
Halligan, Walter 181, 184
Halpin, Capt. 135
Halverstown 86, 182
Hannon, Dennis 97
Hare Park (Curragh) 32, 33, 130, 131, 147, 149, 150, 162, 164, 186
Harrington, Joe 164
Harris, J. 183
Harris, Thomas 14, 20, 21, 23, 27, 61, 62, 76, 102, 110, 111, 112, 116, 123, 134
Harris, William 183
Harristown 100, 117, 137, 158, 191
Harte, C. 65
Hayden, John (Seán) 110, 181
Hazelhatch 146, 193
Heaney, Sylvester 105, 106
Hearty, Liam 164
Heaslip, Comdt 79
Higgins, Jack 171
Higginson, Brigadier General George 37
Hollywood 80, 94
Hollywood, Patrick 183
Horan, Fr 117
Hume, Dick 162
Hunger strikes 15, 150, 161, 162, 163, 164, 165, 166, 167, 178
Hurley, Seán 173

I

International Committee of the Red Cross (ICRC) 152
IRA Convention 69, 77
IRA Executive 63, 68, 69, 157, 164
IRA (Irish Republican Army) 13, 14, 18, 22, 23, 24, 25, 27, 28, 32, 34, 37, 39, 40, 41, 42, 44, 46, 49, 50, 53, 54, 58, 59, 60, 62, 63, 64, 68, 69, 71, 72, 74, 79, 80, 81, 82, 83, 84, 85, 86, 87, 91, 92, 94, 95, 96, 98, 100, 101, 102, 104, 105, 106, 110, 119, 122, 123, 125, 127, 130, 136, 137, 139, 145, 154, 155, 156, 159, 161, 164, 167, 170, 171, 172, 174, 175, 176, 177, 178, 179
Irish Citizen Army 20
Irish Independent 45, 150

Irish Times 39
Irish Volunteers 19, 20, 21, 22, 23, 26, 27
ITGWU 23

J

James, Fr 64
Johnston, Joseph 126
Johnston, Joseph (Jackie) 122, 123, 125, 128, 129, 131
Johnstown 134, 135
Joyce, Capt. John 32

K

Kavanagh, James 183
Kavanagh, Patrick 181
Kavanagh, Seán 26, 27
Kealy, Tom 97
Kearney, John 47, 49
Kells 82
Kelly, Capt. Patrick 22, 60, 134
Kelly, James 182
Kelly, Joseph 123
Kelly, Patrick 181
Kelly, Peter (Corduff) 181
Kelly, Peter (Prosperous) 183
Kelly, Thomas 183
Kenny, Comdt 98, 100
Kenny, James 181
Kent, David 163
Keogh, Lieut John 135
Keredern 41
Kerry 86, 111, 121, 127, 151, 170, 171
Kilbride camp 62, 63
Kilbride, Denis 21
Kilcock 24, 25, 66, 68, 76, 77, 91, 93, 104, 110, 111, 116, 156, 182, 184, 186
Kilcullen 21, 78, 81, 85, 93, 94, 110, 117, 156, 171, 172, 181, 182, 183, 184, 189, 193
Kildangan 137, 189, 191
Kildare barracks 34, 38, 49, 50
Kildare Brigade 27, 81
Kildare Brigade IRA 36, 62, 69, 72, 74, 78, 79, 87, 101, 116, 134, 156, 158
Kildare depot 50, 52, 54, 55
Kildare flying column 23, 24, 86, 92, 102
Kildare Mutiny 44, 48, 49, 51, 54, 55, 56, 57
Kildare Observer 31, 32, 33, 35, 39, 40, 46, 65, 67, 72, 80, 87, 124, 186, 187, 191
Kildare town 14, 17, 18, 20, 29, 30, 32, 37, 39, 41, 42, 54, 57, 82, 94, 123, 168, 174
Kildoon 41, 42
Kilkenny 59, 64, 150, 162
Kill 19, 20, 22, 23, 43, 62, 78, 81, 83, 93, 94, 101, 134, 138, 156, 182, 183, 184, 185, 187, 188, 189, 192
Killeen Bridge 100
Kilmainham Gaol 88, 105, 106, 134, 160, 162, 164, 171, 185
Kilteel 22, 94, 96, 138, 182, 183
Kilwogan 105
Kinahan, Lady Coraile 145
King, John 182
Kingsbridge station 47
Knight, Joseph 181
Knocknacree 99

L

Labour Party 21, 36, 61, 70, 71, 83
Lacey, Joseph 165
Lambe, Maurice 109, 181, 184
Lambe, Peter 181
Laois 20, 167
Lawler, Capt. 70
Lawler, Comdt Peter 86, 87
Lawler, Brigadier Thomas 32, 60, 62
Lawler, William 83
Leinster 58, 66, 84, 110, 138
Leinster House 14, 101, 102, 119
Leinster Leader 24, 34, 35, 60, 67, 115, 128, 150

Leinster Lodge 42
Leinster Rally 64
Leinster Regiment 82
Leixlip 20, 22, 76, 97, 101, 103, 105, 107, 108, 167, 183, 185, 186, 192
Lemass, Noel 168, 169
Lemass, Seán 78, 85, 174
Letterkenny 46
Liddy, Farrell 55
Liddy, Seán 51
Liffey 24, 89, 112, 113, 114, 123
Limerick 14, 17, 18, 59, 111
Limerick Bridge 42
Lloyd George, David 21, 28
Loughbrown 101
Louth 92, 106, 123
Lucan 77, 84, 103
Lumville 22, 137
Lynam, Kit 110, 111, 112, 116
Lynam, Thomas 181
Lynam, Vice-Comdt 103
Lynch, Comdt Martin 45
Lynch, Liam 69, 78, 94, 138, 139, 156, 157
Lynch, Pte Patrick 154

M

Mack, Joseph 170
Mackey, James 109, 181
Mack, Joseph 171
MacMahon, Seán 173
MacNeill, Eoin 119
Maddenstown 23, 110
Magee, Patrick 92, 93
Maher, Jeremiah 26, 45, 46, 50, 51
Maher, Joe 172
Mahon, General Sir Bryan 15, 136, 137, 143, 144, 152
Mahon, Fr 127
Malone, Éamonn 20
Malone, Simon 64
Mangan, Alfred 184
Mangan, Patrick 122, 123, 126, 129, 131

Mangan, Thomas 182
Mannion, Comdt Paddy 96
Markievicz, Countess C. 75
Martin, Joseph 181, 185, 186
Martin, Patrick 181, 185
Maryborough prison 87, 88, 170
Masterson, E. 185
May, Hester 34, 74
May, Joe 34
Maynooth 18, 19, 20, 22, 23, 24, 33, 77, 96, 97, 103, 167, 182, 185, 186, 190, 192
Mayo 47, 50, 51, 101, 108, 138
Mayo, Earl of 15, 136, 137, 138, 139, 140, 141, 143, 159, 187, 189
Mayo, Lady 139, 140, 141, 187
McAvinue, Sgt Patrick 53
McCabe, Thomas 184
McCaul, James 184
McCoy, John 91, 94
McDermott, George 82
McDonnell, Andy 62, 78
McDonnell, Brigadier 104
McDonnell, Comdt Dan 127
McEvoy, Thomas 123
McFaul, John 47
McGarr, Larry 88
McGlynn, Cpl George 101
McGrath, Joseph 64, 67, 119, 173
McKelvey, Joseph 119, 121
McKenna, Michael 55
McKenna, Thomas 182
McLoughlin, Alfred 150, 151
McMahon, Peader 21
McMahon, Thomas 109
McNamara, James 181
McNamara, Sgt Patrick 53
McNeil, Neil 63
McNulty, Comdt 79, 80
Meath 23, 62, 92, 93, 97, 101, 103, 105, 106, 116, 117, 172
Meath flying column 23, 102
Melia, Bernard 181
Melia, James 182
Melia, Thomas 182
Mellows, Liam 73, 119, 121

Metcalf, A. 77
Mid-Kildare Brigade 78
Milbanke, Lady 144
Mills, Christopher 182, 185, 186
Mills, Peter 93, 182
Milltown Bridge 167, 170
Mitchell, E. 93
Mitcheson, W. J. 143, 144
Monasterevin 48, 57, 70, 73, 74, 79, 83, 88, 136, 156, 181, 183, 184, 185, 186, 187, 188, 189, 190
Moore, Annie 125, 127, 133, 134, 177, 185
Moore, Bryan 14, 122, 123, 126, 127, 130, 131, 133, 177
Moore, Pat 123, 127
Mooresbridge 122, 123, 124, 127, 129, 177
Moortown 181, 189
Moran, Edward 77
Moran, Pte Joseph 104
Mountjoy Jail 67, 73, 74, 76, 107, 119, 121, 133, 134, 151, 152, 161, 162, 164, 171, 184, 185
Moyanna 66
Moyvalley 64
Mulcahy, Richard 24, 44, 58, 59, 88, 89, 91, 94, 95, 119, 149, 150, 155, 163, 173
Mullaboden 15, 136, 137, 143, 145
Mullaney, Patrick 14, 76, 77, 97, 101, 102, 103, 105, 106, 107, 108, 167, 185, 186
Munster 138, 154
Murphy, James 99, 100
Murphy, Michael 185, 186
Murphy, Patrick 175
Murphy, Thomas 97, 184, 185, 186
Murray, Capt. James 168, 169, 170
Murray, Pte James 101
Murray, Michael 169
Myers, Henry 109, 181

N

Naas 14, 17, 18, 19, 20, 22, 26, 27, 29, 30, 31, 32, 33, 34, 35, 36, 39, 41, 42, 45, 48, 56, 57, 59, 60, 61, 62, 64, 65, 68, 72, 77, 79, 80, 81, 84, 85, 86, 87, 88, 89, 92, 94, 97, 100, 101, 103, 104, 110, 116, 117, 122, 135, 137, 138, 140, 141, 144, 145, 146, 154, 155, 156, 157, 158, 171, 175, 181, 182, 183, 184, 185, 186
Narraghmore 181, 183
National Army 14, 15, 24, 33, 36, 40, 48, 50, 51, 57, 58, 59, 62, 63, 64, 69, 70, 71, 72, 73, 75, 77, 78, 79, 80, 81, 82, 83, 84, 85, 86, 87, 88, 89, 90, 92, 94, 96, 97, 98, 99, 100, 101, 102, 103, 104, 105, 106, 117, 124, 126, 127, 134, 135, 136, 142, 143, 144, 145, 147, 148, 152, 154, 155, 156, 157, 158, 159, 161, 167, 168, 170, 171, 172, 173, 174, 176, 177, 179
National Army mutiny 57, 173, 174
Navan 82, 106
Neligan, Patrick 185
Newbridge/Droichead Nua 14, 15, 17, 18, 20, 22, 23, 25, 26, 29, 30, 33, 34, 35, 36, 40, 42, 48, 50, 54, 55, 57, 68, 70, 73, 78, 80, 85, 88, 100, 101, 109, 110, 111, 112, 114, 116, 117, 118, 120, 123, 126, 133, 137, 142, 152, 156, 158, 162, 163, 164, 172, 173, 175, 181, 182, 183, 184, 185, 188
Nolan, Lieut Edward 98, 100
Nolan, Michael 186
Nolan, Patrick 122, 123, 126, 130, 131, 132, 133, 177
Nolan, Comdt Seán 81, 82
Noone, Fred 184
Norris, Fr 64
North Dublin Union 134, 162, 185
Northern, Capt. Ernest 42, 136, 188

O

O'Boyle Plunkett, Neil 158
O'Brien, Patrick 182
O'Brien, Peter 184
O'Carroll, Patrick 62, 63, 181, 184, 186
O'Connell, General J. J. 'Ginger' 33, 34, 59, 71
O'Connor, Art 14, 21, 28, 29, 59, 68, 70, 74, 75, 76, 145, 160, 167
O'Connor, Art 185
O'Connor, B. 94
O'Connor, Fanny 94
O'Connor, Jack 167, 185
O'Connor, James (Ballitore) 182
O'Connor, James (Bansha) 122, 123, 126, 129
O'Connor, James (Kildare town) 184
O'Connor, John 21
O'Connor, Rory 54, 119, 121
O'Connor, Seán 186
O'Connor, Seán (Jack) 145
O'Donnell, Peadar 151
O'Duffy, General Eoin 56, 61, 87
O'Duffy, General Eoin 62
O'Higgins, Kevin 52, 64, 67, 119, 174
O'Higgins, Mrs Kevin 65, 67
O'Keefe, Frank 162
O'Keefe, Jim 93, 110, 111, 112, 116
O'Keefe, Patrick 24, 91, 92, 110, 111, 116
O'Kelly, Michael 182, 185
O'Kelly, Ted 19, 20, 96
Ó Máille, Pádraic 119
O'Malley, Ernie 54, 78, 80, 84, 94, 166, 167, 178
O'Mara, Comdt Peter 150
O'Modhrain, Éamonn 20, 40
O'Neill, Éamonn 72
O'Neill, Jim 20
O'Neill, Michael 167, 185, 186
O'Neill, Mick 92, 102
O'Reilly, John 125
O'Reilly, P. P. 65
O'Reilly, Pte Tony 105, 106

Oriel House 95
O'Rourke, James 182
O'Rourke, Michael 182
O'Sullivan, Andy 163
O'Sullivan, Gearóid 64, 65, 67, 89, 90, 173
O'Toole, Lawrence 182
Owens, Comdt Joseph 135

P

Palmerstown House 15, 136, 137, 138, 139, 140, 141, 144, 159
Patterson, Tommy 65
Pender, Pte 156
Pender, William 182
Perkins, Michael 184
Perkins, William 184
Phelan, P. 64
Phelan, Patrick 71
Phoenix Park 35
Pilkington, Liam 164
Portarlington 57, 190
Portobello barracks 88, 103, 106
Price, Michael 95, 96, 116
Pringle, Peter 171
Prosperous 19, 20, 81, 85, 94, 102, 110, 123, 183, 187
Pro-Treaty (see also Free State) 13, 29, 45, 55, 60, 61, 62, 64, 68, 69, 70, 71, 72, 74, 119, 134, 152, 176
Provisional Government (see also Free State/Pro-Treaty) 13, 29, 32, 33, 36, 37, 38, 44, 51, 52, 58, 64, 69, 72, 83, 96, 97, 119, 120, 148, 154, 176, 177, 178
Punchestown 43
Purcell, D.J. 65

Q

Quinn, Pat 182

R

Rafferty, Capt. Jack 116

Index

Rafferty, Seán 182, 185
Railways 14, 20, 25, 26, 31, 42, 47, 57, 100, 123, 124, 125, 126, 129, 146, 154, 188, 189, 190, 191, 192
  attacks on 19, 95, 100, 103, 124, 146, 154, 159
  bridges 18, 20, 24, 86, 92, 124
Rath camp 15, 147
Rathangan 24, 25, 64, 74, 81, 84, 93, 122, 123, 156, 171, 182, 183, 184, 185, 190
Rathbride 122, 123, 126, 185
Rathbride column 14, 122, 123, 124, 127, 128, 129
Rathcoffey Castle 39
Rathcoole 78
Rathmore 182, 186, 187
Rathmuck 137, 192
Reilly, Thomas 84, 85
Republican courts 22, 74
Republican (see also Anti-Treatyites) 13, 14, 15, 21, 22, 23, 24, 25, 29, 33, 34, 37, 42, 43, 45, 46, 48, 51, 53, 54, 55, 56, 58, 59, 60, 62, 63, 64, 66, 68, 69, 70, 71, 72, 73, 74, 75, 76, 77, 78, 79, 80, 82, 83, 84, 85, 86, 88, 91, 92, 94, 95, 96, 97, 102, 103, 104, 105, 108, 109, 114, 116, 117, 119, 121, 123, 126, 128, 134, 136, 147, 148, 149, 150, 152, 154, 155, 156, 157, 158, 159, 160, 161, 162, 163, 164, 166, 167, 169, 171, 174, 176, 177, 178, 179
Restoration of Order in Ireland Act (ROIA) 148
RIC (Royal Irish Constabulary) 15, 19, 22, 23, 24, 26, 32, 33, 34, 43, 44, 45, 46, 47, 49, 50, 51, 53, 55, 56, 67, 69, 146, 147
Ring, Comdt Joe 47, 50, 51
Ring, General Michael 45
Robertstown 81, 156, 187, 193, 194
Robinson, David 164
Rowan, Dr Laurence 39, 64

Royal Dublin Fusiliers 30, 31, 32
Royal Dublin Society (RDS) 47
Russellstown 136, 187
Ryan, Joseph 185
Ryan, M. 77
Ryan, Michael 182

S

Sallins 19, 20, 22, 26, 86, 100, 101, 185, 186, 188
Saurin, Comdt 104, 105
Sheehan, Joe 117
Sheehan, John 117
Sheehan, Lieut Jim 73, 74, 173
Sheehan, Michael 73, 74, 85, 117, 126, 134, 167, 180, 182, 185
Sheehan, Patrick 40, 185
Sheehy, John Joe 171
Sheehy, Pte Lawrence 105, 106
Sheppard, Sylvester 83
Siney, Patrick 183
Sinn Féin 21, 24, 59, 68, 70, 74, 133, 146, 154, 162, 163, 176, 186
Skreen 92
Sligo 64
Smith, J. 150
Smith, Private 145
Smyth, Michael 21, 22, 36, 61, 74
South Dublin Brigade IRA 62, 78, 156
Special Powers Bill 119
Stack, Austin 68, 75
Staines, Michael 45, 46, 47, 50, 51, 53, 56, 64
Stapleton, Comdt 93
Stapleton, M. 65
Straffan 24, 94, 100, 181, 185, 191, 193
Supple, Inspector 26
Sween, Pte Christopher 154
Sweeney, Laurence 83
Swordlestown 100

T

Tait, Major 137, 138

Tallaght 63
Tara 92
Templemore 59
Thomastown 170
Ticknevin 182, 188
Tierney, Fr 72
Tierney, Paddy 84, 85
Timahoe 68, 84, 85
Tintown 15, 147, 148, 149, 151, 152, 162, 165, 166, 167, 169, 185, 186
Tipperary 64, 78, 84, 122, 126, 162
Tobin, Liam 83, 173
Tracey, Edward 184, 186
Tracey, Michael 185
Tracey, Seán 110
Tracy, Martin 182
Travers, Nicholas 66
Trayner, Capt. 104, 105
Traynor, Oscar 74, 75, 77, 78
Trim 40, 82, 103
Truce 14, 27, 28, 37, 42, 44, 62, 100, 137, 159
Trucers 62, 86, 172, 177
Tullow 84, 85
Twomey, Nicholas 182
Tynan, Liam 185
Tynan, William 184
Tyrell, Timothy 167, 185, 186

U

Ulster 58, 66, 69, 84, 91, 138

V

Valleymount 85, 156
Vaughan, Edward 185

W

Wallace, Lily 185
Walsh, Patrick 46, 49
Walterstown 182
War of Independence 13, 14, 17, 18, 27, 28, 34, 44, 45, 46, 48, 73, 94, 102, 120, 123, 136, 138, 147, 148, 155, 167, 177
Watkins, John 78
Watkins, Tom 63
Wexford 84, 101, 154, 162, 165
Whelan, James 72
White, Jimmy 123, 127
White, Stephen 122, 123, 126, 127, 131
Whitt, Pte 100
Whitty, Joseph 162
Whyte, James 62, 116, 117, 184
Wicklow 20, 21, 28, 29, 62, 63, 70, 71, 78, 85, 100, 156, 158
Williams, T. J. 116
Wilson, Sir Henry 71, 84
Wilson, Richard 71
Wogan Browne, Col Francis 38, 41
Wogan Browne, Lieut John Hubert 37, 38, 40, 41, 42, 128
Woods, Patrick 183, 186
Wynne, James 182

Y

Yeats, W. B. 152

www.ingramcontent.com/pod-product-compliance
Lightning Source LLC
Chambersburg PA
CBHW060818190426
43197CB00038B/1933